Tears of Forced
MARRIAGE

Felicia Idemudia

ISBN: 978-1-4834-5733-8 (sc)
ISBN: 978-1-4834-5731-4 (hc)
ISBN: 978-1-4834-5732-1 (e)

Library of Congress Control Number: 2016913826

Lulu Publishing Services rev. date: 10/10/2016

Contents

Acknowledgments

On behalf of myself and my family, I would like to say a big thank you to the many people who have contributed to this book in one way or another. I have really enjoyed the time that I've spent writing this book. It has been a blessing to me and has increased my knowledge about forced marriage. I am also very grateful for the opportunity to have gotten to know so many people and to have listened to their stories and experiences about forced marriage.

To those who have contributed to this book, you are immensely appreciated. Without your contributions this book would not have been a success.

I'd like to give a special thanks to my family for all of their support and their patience, during the time I spent writing this book.

An additional thank you goes to Team SLE Advertising for providing the illuminating illustrations within this book.

About the Author

My name is Felicia Idemudia. I was born and raised in Edo State of Nigeria. I obtained my elementary and secondary education in Nigeria and then came to Canada in search of a better life and higher education. I obtained diplomas in a community workers program and in grief and bereavement management at George Brown College in Toronto, Ontario. At the time of this writing, I was working as a counselor at Surex Community Center in Toronto.

About This Book

The purpose of writing this book is to create awareness about the lives of girls and boys forced into marriage by their parents, especially by the fathers in some countries, cultures, and communities. It includes advice to fathers and mothers who, for their own selfish reasons, force their children into marrying men and women they do not love.

My message in this book is to discourage forced marriages in general and to bring to light the different kinds of forced marriage and the devastating results forced marriage can have. Though many forced into monogamous marriages have problems, those forced into polygamous marriages experience a more negative impact.

People who have grown up in civilized societies and have not seen or experienced other cultures may consider some points in this book to be old-fashioned and no longer relevant. Forced marriage, however, is still a prevalent problem, even in this day and age. Just as poverty is still a major issue in many countries, so too is the issue of forced marriage. Poverty and forced marriage often go hand in hand, and unfortunately, there hasn't been any obvious solution to either issue.

This book gives suggestions as to what can be done to improve the lives of boys and girls affected by forced marriage. Awareness, education, and change are essential if significant improvement is to be made. The people affected by forced marriages are usually weak and vulnerable. They can't stop the process on their own. They need our help in order for things to change.

Note: Most of the names, ages, and locations of the participants mentioned in this book have been changed or withheld to protect their privacy.

About Forced Marriage

Forced marriage was not part of marriage in the beginning of mankind; arranged marriage was. Arranged marriage is a tradition that goes back to biblical times; it was a common practice worldwide. Arranged marriage became problematic, however, when girls started refusing their parents' choices of husbands for them. Due to lack of cooperation from the girls, force was used to ensure that girls married the men their parents chose for them. In North American, a ***shotgun wedding*** is an example of a forced marriage. A shotgun wedding is a marriage in which the couple is forced to marry quickly, regardless of whether the boy or girl involved wants it because the girl is pregnant. This sort of marriage is meant to ensure that the parents (primarily the father) of the girl are not put to shame because of their daughter's unplanned pregnancy and of having a baby out of wedlock.

The father would force the groom at gunpoint to ensure that the man who got his daughter pregnant would follow through with the wedding. Such forced marriages became less popular in North America and in other civilized countries over time.

In many parts of the underdeveloped world, excessive force is more common now than ever in making sure that children marry partners their fathers have chosen for them. Forced marriages are not only used in underdeveloped countries due to pregnancy but for some other reasons as well. Fathers do not only force the couple to marry, but they also force them to remain in the marriage. Girls and boys and men and women in these countries have been crying out for help to escape the brutality of forced marriages, but not enough has been done to help them.

Some stories written in this book are testimonies from people affected by secretly arranged and forced marriages. Other testimonies are from people who have witnessed forced marriage in various parts of the world. Within these pages, I also describe how I almost was a victim of a forced marriage.

I am not writing this book to blame parents who have forced their children into unhealthy marriages in the past; their actions may have been based on their lack of education and cultural practices. I've written this book to encourage parents to give their blessings to their children in their choice of partners

We've all been vulnerable at some point in our lives. We were able to move past the vulnerable periods with the love and support of family and friends who listened, cared, and supported us. Unfortunately, those in forced marriages have been victimized by people who are supposed to help them.

Girls and boys should have the right to choose their wives or husbands. Imagine, for a moment, how it would feel to grow up in what you believed to be a loving family setting, and then suddenly you are sold or shipped to a total stranger at a tender age, just because this is what your parents want for you. Imagining such a situation might give you some understanding of what people in forced marriages have gone through.

The lives of many people in forced marriages are broken and may never be whole again. To help stop the act of forced marriages, you have to listen to the voices of the people affected by it; you need to find out how they are feeling and how their lives have been affected.

This book is also intended to increase awareness about abusive parents, especially fathers, in many cultures and communities. In many communities in Africa, power in the homes is controlled by fathers; mothers have little or no say in the decisions that are made within the household. That being said, this book is not meant to demonize fathers in these cultures, as I know there are many men who are doing a wonderful job of supporting their families. If you are one of those fathers that know the right thing to do, you can help create awareness to others who are not as knowledgeable.

Children in forced marriages are not given the chance to enjoy their lives; many are forced into unhealthy marriages and in toxic environments at an early age. Because of this, they miss out on fun and the most important parts of their lives, such as the teenage years. Can you imagine your own life without your family around to share your joy or sorrow? Can you imagine not having the opportunity to hang out with friends? Well, there are young men and women who can only imagine doing those things.

Parents who force their children into marriages need to understand that they are making their children's lives a living hell. Society needs to understand the negative impact on the victims. With awareness, there may be positive changes. That is the purpose of this book.

The following is a list of feelings expressed by people forced to marry:

- ➢ They feel isolated from their families
- ➢ They feel lost in society
- ➢ They feel lonely
- ➢ They feel scared
- ➢ They feel betrayed by their own parents
- ➢ They feel a lack of trust
- ➢ They feel abandoned
- ➢ They feel vulnerable
- ➢ They feel unwanted
- ➢ They feel their voices are not heard
- ➢ They feel powerless

People who have experienced forced marriages have said that being in a marriage without love is tough. Many girls and women who were forced to marry wondered if they could ever break the cycle of the cruelty inflicted upon them by their husbands. They feel as though they've been sold into slavery by their parents. Many forced to marry have no say in what happens in their lives. Their husbands dictate how they will live their lives. These children are not asking for much; all they want is freedom and to be like other children. Instead of being youths themselves, they watched other youths have fun with their families. They watched as their own families, of which they were supposed to be part, exclude them and move on without them. Some of these children feel they have no family to call their own. They watch in silence as their dreams and goals go down the drain. They are forced to submit to the unwanted men and women that were pushed onto them by their parents.. Once married, regardless of their ages, they are no longer looked at or treated like children; they are expected to know and do everything an adult does.

In some cases, the mental health of these children is affected by early marriages. They become weak and vulnerable. Life passes them by very quickly. Many feel alone, scared, and confused. Children forced to marry go into the marriage with fear, anxiety, confusion, and lack of love, care, and support from their families. Many feel they have no way out and have no one to whom they can turn to.

These children forced into marriages face other problems such as domestic abuse. And in some cases, their culture supports brutality against women, and the law does nothing to support them; girls are afraid to report the crimes.

The police in some of these communities do not take women's reports of domestic abuse seriously. Some of these policemen may be abusive to their own wives and see domestic violence as the norm, and not as a crime. These women are made to understand that violence is a part of their marriage. If they report abuse, they run the risk of further abuse, isolation, and being cut off financially, and they may be denied contact with their children. Instead of being praised for their effort for reporting crimes, they may be crucified for their bravery. Few women escape the hardships of forced marriages. Those who do are left with painful memories that may last forever.

Children affected all over the world need your help to break the cycle of forced marriages. In order to give these children the chance to gain independence and freedom, their voices must be heard. They have to learn what healthy love is. Children have the right to be part of their families and not grow up with a stranger who only wants his or her selfish needs met, regardless of the consequences to the child.

The good news is that many civilized countries like Canada, are helping to break the cycle of forced marriages, especially within their own nations. Many parents exert their control over their children in other countries when they emigrate. Canada is one of the many civilized countries that does not condone the forcing of female children to marry against their will.

The Canadian government is saying no to such practices, and parents found breaking the law face jail sentences. Forcing someone into wedlock is now a criminal offense in Canada, and polygamists are strictly forbidden in this country.

Every year, hundreds of young people are at risk of being taken abroad by their parents to be forced to marry against their will. If there is no help for these children, others will become victims.

The number of forced marriages is alarming. I hope this book will help to create awareness in this situation and bring this practice to an end. I'd like to send a very significant thanks to Canada, America, England, and many other countries that are doing everything in their power to stop this practice; but other countries also need to forbid forced marriages on their soil and make forced marriages a thing of the past.

Introduction

The contributions of the brave men and women who agreed to be interviewed for this book are greatly appreciated, and it will help people to understand that forced marriage is not the best marriage and should never be practiced. Until recently, there have been few books or outreach to promote self-esteem and education for women of forced marriages. These women have had to suffer in silence with no hope and no one to listen to their complaints. They were sometimes considered weak and were criticized if they complained about their husbands' cruel behavior toward them.

Traditional beliefs and attitudes toward child abuse or forced marriages in many parts of Africa is the cause for the increase of such practices. In most cases, little or nothing has been done by individuals or governments to stop these practices.

This book is based on forced marriages in Nigeria, Africa, and some other parts of the world; so it is very important to understand how forced marriages connect with other types of marriages, and how it can lead to spousal abuse. In most cases, it also can lead to child abuse and unhappiness later in these marriages.

Marriage is something most people dream of; but for those in a forced marriage, it can become a nightmare. Marriage is the happiest bond between a man and a woman if they love each other. Because there is no love in a forced marriage, this can lead to negligence, loneliness, unhappiness, spousal abuse, and sometimes death.

Women and children of forced marriages find it difficult to compare their situations with others because they are not in the same space, and the treatment they receive is also different from others. In some cultures, women involved in forced marriages have to join a harem of other wives. These women often have to compete for their men's attention and affection. These women who live as group wives are treated as a collection and not as individuals. Worse yet, their children often suffer the consequences. The more women, the more children, the more limited resources become. In addition, children of the wives who are considered the husband's favorites often get preferential treatment, creating unfair and psychologically damaging circumstances for the other children.

Any parent who forces their daughters into polygamy should think of how their decisions impact the other wives of that marriage and how their selfish decision also negatively impacts their potential grandchildren.

When I spoke to some people in forced marriages, both those who remained in the marriage for various reasons and those who divorced had one thing to say: "It is not a good experience."

Although some people may think that forced marriages are no longer an issue, forced marriages are still a prevalent problem, even in this day and age. At this point, however, there doesn't seem to be any obvious solutions.

CHAPTER 1

Polygamy/Forced Marriage

Polygamy often leads to the abuse of women and children in Africa today. Plural marriages are very common in Africa's history. Many African societies saw children as property; thus, the more children a family had, the more powerful it was.

Polygamy is still a common practice in most parts of African countries, especially among poor families who rely on their daughters as their source of income and use them to assist in building their family's wealth. Fathers from these cultures marry their daughters to wealthy men; some with other wives, at an early age; as young as twelve. In some parts of Africa, girls are forced to marry by the time they are between thirteen and seventeen years old. Polygamy was part of the empire-building in some countries and still is. Children are not only seen as property, they also are seen as a retirement plan and their parents' insurance.

Many parents do not have any form of insurance. Some can't afford it, but they also do not think it is necessary. These parents see it as their children's moral obligation to financially care for them in their old age. Parents in these cultures typically rely on their sons, especially their eldest sons, to make sure that their transition into their senior years is a smooth one.

When the eldest child is a daughter or when there are no male children, it becomes even more urgent for parents to marry off their daughters as soon as possible for quick profits and so their sons-in-laws can stand in for the sons they never had. They hope these sons will bring wealth to their families and give them grandsons to continue their family names. Parents view their daughters' early marriages as a blessing. It is a way to preserve family honor, and they believe that it guarantees that their daughter will remain a virgin until she is married off. They believe that early marriage corrects children's behaviors. They also see rich in-laws as bringing wealth to them.

These families look out for themselves when making the decision to marry their daughters to wealthy men. They turn their eyes away from the dangers their daughters may have to face. Some claim it is the right thing to do.

Even today, parents in African families who believe in children marriages cannot be convinced of the dangers involved. They believe that going against this practice will make their traditions obsolete. For them, the tradition of early marriage and polygamy is an important part of their culture. They see men with plural wives as being responsible. Although some women go into polygamy by choice for the financial and material benefits, most young women do not look forward to entering into a polygamous relationship.

If you are a woman from a society where polygamy is still practiced and have chosen to enter such a marriage, please consider the situation you are getting yourself into, as well as your own motives for wanting to be involved in such a scenario. The decision you make in this regard may seem to only impact you, but there are others; including the other wives, their children, and your children, who will be affected by your choice. I personally object to polygamous marriages, but if people choose to practice polygamy in their own countries, they must take a hard look at themselves and examine their strengths; both financially and emotionally.

Below are some things a man should consider before he practices polygamy or plural marriage:

> ➢ You must be able to provide for your family, both emotionally and financially

- ➤ You must be able to cope with your family's demands
- ➤ You must love your wives as you love yourself
- ➤ You must love them equally
- ➤ You must care for them equally
- ➤ You must spend equal time with them
- ➤ You must be able to deal with arguments and resolved conflict
- ➤ You must be able to provide education for all your children; both sons and daughters
- ➤ You must spend an equal amount of time with all your children
- ➤ You must be fair in your judgment toward your children
- ➤ You must not depend on your father for financial support to provide for your children
- ➤ You must not regard your wife as your property and your children as just numbers
- ➤ You must be respectful to your wives and children.
- ➤ You must regard your wives and children as your highest earthly loyalty
- ➤ You must put their needs above all needs and please them before other people
- ➤ You must not put the burden of raising your children, financially or emotionally, on your wives or family members
- ➤ You must be man enough to shoulder all your responsibilities

If you are not able to provide your family with the above, you have to seriously consider if plural marriage is for you. Realistically, when one man is dealing with many wives and a multitude of children, he does not have the time to pay adequate attention to his wives and children, to give them the basic things in life, or meet the expectations of a responsible father.

This book is not meant to break up couples who are already in forced marriages but to help men identify their behaviors and attitudes toward their wives and children and to consider options to treat their wives and children with love and respect. In every person, there are good and bad behaviors. If you focus on the good behaviors, the bad ones will disappear with time.

However, there are very few success stories about forced marriages; these are not without fights and pain. If you are already in a forced marriage, it is okay to try to make the best of your situation, but it is not advisable to pass on the practice to your children simply because you have been through it. There are more complications involved with forced marriages than benefits, particularly for the women and children involved. Because men do not suffer from nearly as many of the negative aspects involved with forced marriage; they often cannot fully grasp the danger. Women suffer the consequences in most cases, and men seem to not understand the impact it has on women.

There was an old man in our village who was my grandpa's friend. This man was always coming to my grandpa's house to complain about how disappointed he was with his two female children whom he had forced to marry; both their husbands were with plural wives. I asked him one day if he thought his children were having marital problems because he forced them to marry. He looked at me and said, "What do you know about marriage?" He was right. At the time, I knew nothing about marriage, but I knew enough to know that when you force someone to marry against her will, the result is unhappiness. He said that he did not believe there was anything wrong with forced marriage; he felt it was a parent's right to decide whom their daughters or sons should marry. He also believed it was a cultural thing and should be left the way it is.

There are cases of girls forced to marry older men with plenty of property and money. Girls in this situation learn to replace love with money and do not really know what love should be like within a marriage. Most of these girls are controlled by their husbands. They are abused on a daily basis, either physically or verbally, or the man threatens to take away the rich lifestyle that they have come to hold dear. Even with these abuses, these women feel as though they are luckier than other women who marry men who are not rich.

An example of this from my personal experience is a situation that involved a rich man who had several homes, including a mansion, in the area where I grew up. He was already married when he decided to take on a second wife. This second wife was beautiful and very young, nearly twenty-five years younger than he was. She was also twenty years younger than his original wife. Though this young woman became his wife, he treated her as though she was a possession, rather than a person. He was protective, overbearing, and controlling. She was not allowed to work outside of his home, even though she was educated; nor was she allowed to have any friends.

He bought her an expensive car and provided her with other expensive material things, but he controlled her every move, to the point that she was not allowed to be alone in her car. She had to be escorted by a personal driver or a relative of her husband's. When she was allowed out of the house, she was only permitted to wear what he would choose for her. The jewelry that she wore had to be returned to him after each use, even though he bought it for her. He locked it up in a safe in his room, and she could only access it with his permission.

Many women have lost their identity and their voices and are afraid to talk about their experiences. I attempted to interview two women affected by forced marriages during one of my visits to Benin City, Nigeria, some years ago. Both were still married to their respective husbands of forced marriages. One had been married for over twenty five years, and the other had been married for about twenty years. Neither one of them were willing to disclose exact details of their experiences within their marriages, though one did provide some insight by stating, "I would not wish my marriage experience upon my worst enemy. That is all I can say." The other woman seemed to agree with her, nodding her head solemnly. They clearly feared retribution from their husbands if they spoke out against their marriages. Even with the assurance that their names would not be mentioned, they still refused to share specific details. The fears and unhappiness they tried to hide were very evident.

The two women I have briefly described above were not the only women who seemed afraid to speak about the trials and tribulations of their marriages. I had little success with interviewing women of various non-Western cultures. I always tried to ask them open-ended questions to enable them to speak freely about their experiences, but what I got in response, most times, were closed answers.

It is not clear why many young girls become victims of their fathers' actions or why their fathers face no consequences in most cases. Some organizations are now focusing on fathers who use their underage daughters as collateral to settle their debts, as well as focusing on how to stop these acts that have put many young girls in danger; but this practice has deep roots in some communities.

Most parents who force their children to marry often do so for similar reasons, such as:

> - Lack of knowledge
> - Lack of education
> - Poverty
> - Societal beliefs
> - Cultural beliefs and practices
> - Lack of understanding
> - Prestige
> - To protect their children
> - Family respect
> - To promote their culture
> - To carry on ancestral tradition
> - To ensure their female children do not lose their virginity before marriage

I remember once asking my father why he and some of his friends chose men and forced their children to marry. He explained that they did this to maintain their status in the community and to prevent their children from marrying someone from a culture other than their own. He denied that they did it for money or material wealth. He claimed they wanted their children to remain in their own social groups and not lose their identity to other groups. I think this is the same reason why some rich parents force their children to marry into rich families; to retain their wealth within the family.

This may have been true in the past, when men were not as greedy as they are today and when the economy was much better. As the economy has deteriorated, many parents however, deviate from value and are now forcing their children to marry for financial gains.

In African countries affected by AIDS, earthquakes, famine, and drought, these crises further put girls at risk of forced marriages, as parents are desperate. They can no longer care for themselves and their families financially. They force their daughters into marriage at much earlier ages, and some sell their children to wealthy men. Once a girl is forced to marry in this society, she can never seek divorce as long as her husband wants her. She is his stock and she will live a life of misery, because the woman "belongs to" her husband. Some girls are betrothed and then forced to marry before they reach puberty.

Violence against women and young girls is frequent in these societies. The unfortunate thing is that children witness violence against their mothers on a daily basis in their home; it becomes the norm to them because they do not know any other way. Most of them grow up to be violent in their relationships and marriages, which means the cycle continues. Some parents use their daughters as currency to pay debts. Parents see their daughters as objects and as property, and their daughters are used to set the parents free financially.

Domestic violence is one of the main problems in forced marriages. A girl forced to marry at an early age carries a heavy burden; she does not have the ability to deal with the duties of a wife. At her young age, she is mentally, physically, and morally unready to be a wife. This is especially true if she is dealing with other wives, sexual demands, and other overwhelming responsibilities involved in a forced marriage. She may experience depression and lack high self esteem and self-care. The majority of young girls who are unhappy in their marriages face the following:

- Health risks
- Divorce
- Suicide

- Depression
- Abuse
- Controlling husbands
- Mental illness
- Domestic violence
- Abduction
- Unlawful confinement/imprisonment
- Humiliation/shame
- Low self-esteem
- Self harm
- Disappointment
- Lack of education
- Lack of self-care

Most of these young girls have no social status; they are always under their husbands' control, especially in the rural communities where cultural attitudes are strong. These girls are helpless and have no voice. The law and legislation put in place to protect and prohibit forced marriages is not followed in most African countries. The girls cannot fight for themselves and are powerless to defend themselves. Most lack education and their own money.

The few forced marriages that survive generally are less problematic because the girls marry men of their own age groups and are not involved in polygamy. Those who marry older men and/or men with plural wives have a higher rate of divorce, abuse, and lack control of their own lives.

I interviewed some women and a couple of men affected by forced marriages in a city where there are fewer forced marriages and some have found it more beneficial to educate their female children than to force them to marry. The rate of forced marriages is still very high in most villages, and the village women I interviewed all said the same thing: "forced marriage is not a good experience." Some organizations in the cities educate young women and condemn the act of forced marriages; but this is lacking in the villages.

Some of the women I interviewed responded willingly, but most of the men I interviewed refused to answer questions and believed that the interview was unnecessary. I tried to explain the difference between marriage by choice, to someone you love and forced marriage. Some men stated it is all the same, and it does not matter how you marry a woman or what form it takes. "A wife is a wife", the said.

A forced marriage should not be confused with an arranged marriage. An arranged marriage is done with the knowledge and agreement of both the man and the woman and can be beneficial to both. Arranged marriages are "pre-planned," which means that a parent, friend, or well-wisher introduces a husband for a woman and a wife for a man with the knowledge of both.

A forced marriage means that parents choose a spouse for their sons or daughters and set the date for the marriage without their children's knowledge or permission. The parents receive a "bride price". Even if the girls object to their parents' choices, their objections are always ignored, and their marriages take place regardless. Sometimes girls are forced to marry men who are old enough to be their fathers or even grandfathers.

Often the girls are forced to marry abusive husbands, and they are abused, beaten, and neglected on a daily basis. They have no power to free themselves; their power has been taken away by their own fathers, who are supposed to protect them from harm. Even when their fathers are aware of the abuse, they cannot remove the girls from the situation because they have received a bride price and cannot afford to return it. For this reason, the girls are left in the abusive home to continue their suffering. In some cases, they are subjected to slavery by their husbands and in-laws.

Arranged Marriage

An arranged marriage is the union of a man and woman that is brought about by someone other than the bride and groom. Historically, it was the primary way in which future spouses were selected, and it still is a fairly common practice in certain parts of the world today. This may or may not lead to marriage. In arranged relationships, people have the choice to marry or not to marry the person introduced to them. They have the time to get to know each other, and love may or may not develop. Many centuries ago, it was a practice worldwide, including in Jewish history, for fathers to select wives for their sons and husbands for their daughters from the country or city of their origin; but force was not used. This was also the practice in biblical times. In Genesis 24, Abraham, the servant of God, sent one of his own servants to "his country, his father's people, to his relatives, [to] choose a wife for his son."

The servant that was in charge of Abraham's property took ten of his master's servants and camels and went to the city, where he met Rebecca, who became the wife of Abraham's son Isaac. This is to say that arranged marriage existed way back to Bible times (Genesis 24:3, 10; 38:6).

Sometimes, proposals were initiated by the father of the maiden. The brothers of the maiden were also sometimes consulted, but her own consent was not required and her feelings didn't matter. Today, in the civilized world, arranged marriages must consult the prospective bride and groom, and both have a say about it.

In most marriages, someone else gets two people together, whether by phone, by e-mail, or by direct invitation to a special place where they can meet each. Sometimes the person looking for a mate asks for help from a friend or family member in arranging a meeting with someone.

Say for example, you are interested in someone, but you are not sure how to approach the person, you can ask someone who is known by or is close to the person to arrange a meeting to bring the two of you together. There is nothing wrong with doing this.

As the relationship progresses, it will be up to the two people to decide on whether they wish to get married or not. If both decide to get married, they are involved in the planning process and have the choice to invite whoever they want to attend their wedding. They are fully involved in every arrangement of their wedding.

The person who brings the two people together does so with the best intentions. If their relationship progresses positively, and both gets to know each other very well and agree to marry each other, it is perfectly fine. They love first and then marry; this is the Western custom. In African culture, it was marriage first and love later. This still stands today, in many cultures.

Only in recent, in some parts of Africa, has the influence of the Western culture and Christianity led to women being able to choose their own husbands.

Christianity played a big part in trying to put a stop to forced marriages. As Christianity expanded over the years, women and men were given the freedom to choose their own spouse or partner, though there is still some form of arranged/forced marriages within some Christian populations. In countries without the influence of Christianity, forced marriages is on the increase. Many churches today, including Roman Catholic churches, do not accept the practice of forced marriages.

Before the influence of the Western world and Christianity, forced marriage was prevalent in all cultures. The duty of a woman and her daughter was to remain under the dictatorship of the father and husband; in all cases, fathers arranged marriages. If the father died before a daughter reached the age of marriage, the responsibility of choosing a husband for her went to the uncle or another prominent male member of her family. She must not communicate or make decisions on her own.

For a woman to look in her husband's eyes was regarded as disrespectful in some cultures. Women looked down instead of looking straight at their husbands. This is still very much in practice in some of the developing world. Basically, women are not allowed to have minds of their own. They remain quiet and bottle things in.

A quiet woman that does what she is asked, is believed to be a sign of an obedient woman, and female children do exactly as their mothers do, which is also considered a sign of good children. Husbands treat both wife and daughter as children; they forever remain children. From the day a woman is born, she is treated like a thing in some cultures, and the same treatment continues even when she is grown up. A female child is under the control of her father, and when she is married, she is under her husband's control and power. The control and power the husband has over her is forever. It is like going from the frying pan into the fire.

The following are some reasons parents gave as benefits of forced marriages:

- It promotes cultural beliefs
- It keeps people together within the same society
- It gives parents control over their children or family members
- It enables parents to have control of their wealth
- It unites two families
- It enables elders to mediate between couples if there are any marital problems; instead of going to court
- It enables parents to better know the family of their children's spouse

Regardless of parents' explanations, many people in civilized countries view this practice as a barbaric act against women, and they condemn the rigid ways in which forced marriages are conducted. It is described as a one-way traffic; it does not give people involved in these marriages the option to say no, and it creates dependency for the women on their husbands. It takes away women's freedom and choices.

It is an ongoing battle to change the minds of the old-fashioned fathers who believe in rigid tradition. Some organizations are trying to encourage fathers who forced their children into marriage to listen to their cries and voices. As long as this practice continues, the battle for freedom for most girls is still a century away. And without help for them, change may never come.

CHAPTER 3

Forced Marriage — Different from Arranged Marriage

s mentioned earlier, forced marriages were not part of the origin of marriage in the beginning. It started as a result of girls refusing their parents' choices of men for them. Arranged marriages were the only way marriages were conducted. Girls and women relied on their parents' judgment for their husbands, and in all cases, parents were expected to choose a spouse for their children.

Arranged marriages are conducted differently from country to country. Direct or indirect forms of forced marriages became popular across Europe at some point and continued to be practiced to the latter part of the nineteenth century, especially by those in the upper classes. In North America, "shotgun weddings" were practiced into the twentieth century, and forced marriage by religious leaders was not left out. Forced marriages are not particular to a certain religion; it occurs within families: Although most religions prohibit forced marriages directly, families even within some religious communities, continue to practice it.

Forced marriages were stopped altogether in most civilized countries after a long time of practice, as the negative impact became obviously destructive to boys, girls, men, and women in forced marriages. Parents in civilized countries gave their children freedom to choose their own husbands and wives. Forced marriages are still very much in practice in most undeveloped, uncivilized, poor countries and societies.

In some uncivilized countries, this also includes selling their children for quick money. Selling of children mostly affects underage girls, and in some cases, parents are forcing their young girls into the prostitution industry. Some parents are forcing and selling their children as young as eleven years old for little money. This has been common practice in many African countries due to lack of education and poverty.

Parents that are caught in this act often blame their acts on poverty; this is a common excuse given by many parents who had sold their children, forced them into prostitution, sold them into slavery, or forced them to marry against their will for other financial gains.

In some African countries, forced marriages are not peculiar to a specific culture or society. Anyone can be a target of a forced marriage, regardless of gender, race, culture, occupation, religion, physical mental abilities, or personalities. It is more common in some religions and societies than in others. Girls are more vulnerable than boys. Poverty, ignorance, and lack of education are reported to be a major factor.

Most people who still practice this are poor, lack education, and are often unemployed. They may lack awareness, and because of their upbringing, they don't see it as wrong. Some rich parents also practice forced marriages to retain their status and for business and political reasons.

In some forced marriages, girls are tortured to ensure they will marry their parents' choice of men, and they may be taken abroad without knowing that their marriages have been arranged with foreign men. Sometimes the parents seize the girls' passports and other documents to keep them in the foreign country.

Forced marriages, even when it leads to death, are not treated as a crime in countries that still practice it. To some, it is considered the societal norm. Criminal penalties, however, are more effective, because domestic violence is a crime. Abusers should be held accountable, but this doesn't happen in most cases. Forced marriages are a breach of human rights; it is abuse, a crime, and leads to domestic violence; but even then, it is not taking seriously by the law in most African countries.

Indirect Form of Forced Marriage

There is another indirect form of forced marriage; this is where a father, mother, or close relation makes the decision and selects a wife or husband for the son or daughter. They make arrangements to solidify things based on their own choices, and then they make their choice known to their sons or daughters. This mostly happens in rich families. Even if their daughter or son does not like or agree with their choices, many of them are forced to go along with it for financial reasons and because they do not want to disobey or disappoint their parents. In this case the father or the person who selects the wife is responsible for paying the bride price, which in some cases can be very expensive, depending on the tradition.

Since children are at the mercy of their parents, especially their fathers, and they have no money of their own and nowhere to run, many have no choice but to obey their parents to avoid bodily harm. Even with the civil law now in many parts of Africa, which is meant to protect females from being forced to marry, the law is not enforced. Many parents are still forcing their daughters to marry; this is on the rise. Some parents claim it is their right to have full control over their children, and they ignore government law. They believe that their children belong to them and not to the government or other protective groups; therefore, they feel they can do whatever they want with their children.

Slavery in Forced Marriage

Forced marriage is a form of enslavement. Many girls and young women may have been sentenced to slavery because of forced marriages every year. Some may have been sentenced to death in the same name. Forced marriages need to be eliminated worldwide, to stop the killings of innocence children by their parents and husbands. Many girls in forced marriages are in bondage. To be in bondage does not only mean that you are in shackles, chains, or locked up in jail.

In some marriages, it means rejection, hatred, mind control, lack of freedom of speech, and lack of movement. Very often, people think of slavery as a thing of the past, but when you look closely at the girls, boys, men, and women affected by forced marriages and the way they are been treated, you will see that forced marriages is a form of slavery; it is a corrupt form of marriage.

The treatment that girls and women forced to marry receive from their husbands is no different from what the slaves got from their masters. In forced marriages, girls and women spend their lives in bondage without freedom

Husbands know that these girls are helpless. They treat them like commodities, like kitchen utensils, and some turn them into baby-making machines and sex objects. They treat them like second-class citizens, turning them into punching bags and sometimes killing them. Some die of broken hearts or premature death. All these are very common in forced marriages. Forced marriages can be a one-way ticket to a place of no return, a way to disaster and sometimes death. Those who survive are left with scars and memories that will haunt them for the rest of their lives.

Many believe that forced marriages only happen in the villages or rural areas; others believe that civilization and education has reduced or stopped the act of forced marriage. This is not the case; as a matter of fact, it is on the increase.

Forced Marriage Is Not a Thing of the Past

Most people from civilized countries, where forced marriages does not exist, may wonder if forced marriage is still in existence and who is affected by it. It is still very much in existence, and it affects people from all over the world, with the exception of developed countries. It is even secretly practiced in the civilized world by people who migrate to those countries and bring their traditions with them. It is mostly practiced in Africa, Asia, and the Middle East and is more commonly practiced by some cultures than others. It affects people from all religions as well as a variety of backgrounds. It is more widespread than you can imagine.

In countries where arranged and forced marriages are practiced, parents believe that they are doing the right thing to secure their children's future by marrying them to the wealthy, respectful, and responsible families they choose; they believe it will prevent divorce and broken marriages. They also claim the reason for the high divorce rate in many civilized countries today is because people put love before marriage. People marry for love, without checking the background of their husbands or wives. They also believe divorce rates are low in the cultures that practice arranged and forced marriages. This may be true to their beliefs, but I think the reason divorce rate is low in these societies is because women of forced marriages have no rights, no say, and no control of what happens in their lives. They stay in the marriages for many other reasons. In the countries where the divorce rates are high, women have the right to divorce if the marriage is unhealthy and dangerous. These women believe it is better to be free and single than to be married and unhappy.

Girls affected by forced marriages find it very hard to refuse and are not even given the chance to refuse. The society they grow up in encourages such behavior, and this makes it even more difficult for them to escape forced marriages. Forced marriages are not peculiar to illiterates; it also affects some educated boys and girls, but it is more common among illiterates. Some young educated girls from many parts of Africa have been deceived by their parents to, for example, when they are told to come home for an urgent issue. Once they get home, they are then told by their parents or guardians that their marriages have been arranged. In some cases, their traveling documents are seized, and they are forced to marry against their will. With awareness of resources and education, some of these girls were able to contact the authorities and get help; others were not so lucky.

Many girls forced to marry felt they have been let down by society and even feel that God is not listening to their prayers. The fact is that God did not put them in bad situations or allow bad things to happen to them. The choices men made brought the consequences to their actions; unfortunately, this affects their children who are not part of their decisions. God does not mean to hurt his children. Some wondered, then, why it appeared that God was not listening to them.

Remember that teachers are quiet during a test. In your struggles, God gave you the strength to be the strong person you are. Pray, and do not give up hope, and believe there is light after dark. Use the strength God gave you to hold on. As a woman, God gave you an amazing strength.

You may be in the dark place right now, heartbroken, and you may feel unloved. You may be struggling to survive and wondering if you will ever be out of your bondage. Don't be discouraged because brokenness is not the end of your life. As they say, "A downfall of a man is not the end of his life." Keep believing in yourself and continue to pray, and God will answer your prayer when you least expect it, at the right time.

Some cultures hold strongly to customs and traditions and are afraid to let go, as letting go would mean losing power. For those who strongly believe in tradition, it is easier for them to kill their daughters in the name of honor than to break away from the tradition. In many cultures, most girls are married by the time they are fourteen or fifteen. If she is not yet in her husband's house in this culture, she may be already betrothed to a man.

The culture and society they grown up in promote early marriage and girls' virginity. It is impossible for girls to get their freedom when society considers it a norm, and many of these girls do not know any better. These children are not involved in what happens in their lives because they do not get asked for their opinion. Their mothers do not get asked either; they are not allowed to take part in the decisions that affect their children because they are "just" women.

By marrying children at early ages, families put them in situations of isolation, health problems, abuse, suicide, and lack of education. These parents believe they are doing what is best for their children, and they do not consider the negative impact it will have on their young girls. Parents use so many methods of harsh punishment to force their children into marriage, including threatening behavior, emotional blackmail, and physical violence; the children may be killed in some cases if they refuse.

Poverty is another reason why girls are forced to marry at a very young age. Poor parents marry their children to repay debts and to feed the family. Some girls who are forced to marry are indebted for life. In some cases, they are passed on to another member of their husband's family if their husband dies. In some parts of Africa, widows sometimes marry the brothers of their dead husbands and sometimes their brothers-in-law, to get moral and financial support for her children. A man who marries his late brother's wife, and society accepts it, often believes he is not doing anything wrong. Some claim they are following the practice of the ancient time, as written in the Bible.

> If two brothers live on the same property and one of them
> dies, leaving no son, then his widow is not to be married

to someone outside the family; it is the duty of the dead man's brother to marry her. The first son that they have will be considered the son of the dead man, so that his family line will continue in Israel. But if the dead man's brother does not want to marry her, she is to go before the town leaders and say; "my husband's brother will not do his duty; he refuses to give his brother a descendant among the people of Israel." Then the town leaders are to summon him and speak to him. If he still refuses to marry her, his brother's widow is to go to him in presence of the town leaders, take off one of his sandals, spit in his face, and say, this is what happens to the man who refuses to give his brother a descendant. (Deuteronomy 25:5–10)

His family will be known in Israel as the family of the man who had his sandal pulled off.

Even worse, now in some communities, when a man commits a crime, his sister is forced to marry her brother's victim as a way to pay for the crime her brother committed against the victim.

And it is very difficult for them to be civilized. People like these need help to be educated and to make them realize that times have changed. Things are not done the same as in the ancient times. There is strong evidence in many African countries that many people still hold on strongly to their destructive traditional beliefs. Lots of these people also practice polygamy. They believe they are doing women a favor by engaging in plural marriages. Others claimed they are doing it to give women status, to provide for their economic needs, and to protect them. Some do not have a good reason for practicing plural marriages; they do it just because they saw their father doing it.

Most girls forced to marry are abused daily by their husbands and the husband's family members. They have no financial means and are too weak and too afraid to report an abuse. Sometimes when help comes to them, it is too late; the damage has been done.

In some cases when a girl is bold enough to report her ordeal to the authorities, surprisingly the police turn her away and ask her to settle her matter with her husband. They regard this as a domestic issue, which is not taken seriously in this society. The fact that men are never wrong when it comes to domestic issues makes matters worse for women. When a husband kills his wife in a domestic fight, it is like he is destroying a piece of his property that he no longer needs, and nothing comes out of it. The lack of action by the police further subjects the girls to abuse and further scares them away from reporting the abuse. Women are not protected, as the laws are not enforced.

In some communities, if a girl ran away and she is captured by her husband or husband's family, she can be severely punished by her husband. As punishment, the husband can disfigure her by setting her on fire until she is partially burnt; or cut off her hand, ear, or nose so that no other man would ever marry her. The way the society views marriages and the control men have over their wives gives them the power to treat their women as their properties. Some men do this because they can get away with it and most especially because there is no love between them and the women they killed. No one would ever treat someone he loves in this manner.

Healthy marriage is related to love; there is no good or healthy marriage without love. Some men who entered into a forced marriage claimed there was no need to love; some stated they would try to love after marriage, and some others stated they only married so the woman (or women) could bear them children. It is no surprise that these men do not know how to love their children, especially their female children. A man must love his wife first in order to extend his love to his child or children. Marriage should not be on a trial basis but on true love. Love needs to be shared always, anywhere you go with your wife or husband, in public and private and should last forever, not only for a short time, not for days, weeks, months or years, but until death do you part." A good marriage relationship should increase as you grow older and continue through your golden years. You were attracted to each other at a young age and should be attracted to each other through old age and wrinkles, in sickness and in health.

Forced marriages are damaged before they reach old age. In most cases, when there was no attraction to each other at the beginning, there likely won't be attraction to each other in old age, especially those who were forced into polygamy. Many women who survive forced marriages are at their children's mercy in their old age. They look forward to their children caring for them. A husband, who did not care for his wife when she was young, will not care for her when she is old, especially if her husband has plural wives. If her children neglect her in her old age, she may die early, as she cannot support herself financially.

Forced marriages are not one of the social institutions under which a man and a woman establish a relationship and decide to live with one another, for better or for worse, until death do them part, as is written in the Bible. "Leave your father and mother and become one flesh." Forced marriage is not committed to one flesh, as they mostly live individual lives under the same roof. Such marriages have no solid commitment, which makes it difficult to live together as one flesh. Some African men find it difficult to leave their father and mother and live with their wives as one flesh; instead, they bring their wives into their family homes. Some who left their father and mother do not necessarily become one flesh with their wives; they take with them their learned, primitive, controlling behavior and live as cat and rat with their wives.

As men and women were created to be with each other, they were each given a role to play in the marriage. The apostles stated clearly and enforced the important duties of husband and wife in Peter 3:1–7.

For a man, his wife will become his responsibility. He is to love her and give her tender care and affection. He is to please her before any other person, even his own parents. He is to be committed to her. Husband and wife are joined together by God; they are now one flesh. They are expected to live together forever as one and do things together. They are to stick together, for better or for worse, until death do them part. A man is to protect and lead his wife, as he is the head of his wife and family. A man must live up to his God-given responsibility.

On the other hand, a woman must respect her husband, as stated by the apostle Paul in Ephesians 5:33. "When you respect your husband you reverence him, notice him, regard him, honor him, prefer him, and esteem him. It means valuing his opinion, admiring his wisdom and character, appreciating his commitment to you, and considering his needs and values."

For this to happen, however, the man must first show his love and true leadership to his wife and family.

His leadership as head of the family must be displayed with love and in consideration of his wife and of his family's needs.

He should never be a dictator to his wife. He is not to take his wife for granted and enslave her.

His wife should be treated with respect and not be taken advantage of or treated as a common commodity.

He must show his good leadership to his wife and children with words and actions.

Forced Marriages are NOT Okay.

It is not okay to force anyone into marriage, whether a man, woman, boy, or girl.

It is very wrong to secretly arrange a marriage on behalf of anyone and force the person to marry. Forcing a child to marry someone much older, in some cases someone old enough to be her father or grandfather, is not okay. In lots of cases, these children are forced into polygamy and into abusive homes. The decision to choose husbands or wives should be left with girls and boys or men and women and not their parents, because they are the ones to live with each other. As they say, "He who wears shoes knows where it hurts."

Parents who force their children to marry in many countries call it tradition or culture. No good tradition or culture should promote forced marriages. It leads to wife and child slavery or abuse because that is what forced marriages are. When parents force their daughters or sons into marriage, they are indirectly forcing the daughter into abuse, neglect, slavery, isolation, emotional withdrawal, violence, hatred, and hostility. It is all connected.

Traditionally, polygamy is encouraged and accepted in lots of countries, and it is legal, except in the Christian religion. Traditionally, in some cultures, a man can marry as many wives as he wants and have as many children as he wants, regardless of his ability or inability to take care of them. Children brought up by these inconsiderate parents end up on the street. Some end up as armed robbers, killers, and uneducated, and some others are left to fend for themselves at an early age. Most of these children are in poverty and are financially and emotionally unstable for the rest of their lives. For many, there is no way out of poverty. This may lead many to unhealthy relationships, and they may not be able to marry, even though their parents and society that failed them want them to get married. They are broken, emotionally, physically, and financially. They find it difficult to have good relationships. When some marry, they are only able to marry someone of their type, "poor." When this happens, the circle of poverty continues; the poor marry the poor and have poor children. Some of these children are not able to marry due to mental damage, even if they are of age to marry.

No one said you cannot have many children, if this is your goal; but you should also make it your goal to properly care for them. Your children are your responsibilities; they should never end up on the street or in a mental institution due to your inability to care for them.

Are All Men Fit to Be Husbands and Fathers?

This is a good question that many people do not ask. In some cultures, people believe that marriage is determined by age. At a certain age, a man's parents and society expect him to marry. Many are not ready and don't know how to be good fathers and husbands. Men are supposed to know their role and responsibilities as husbands and fathers, financially, emotionally, and physically, before they get married. Millions of men around the world are confused as to what their roles are as husbands and fathers and are ashamed to express their insecurity. With some, control is their way of covering up their insecurities; they exercise this control over their family. The problem is that many do not learn how to be mature, responsible, and secure husbands when they are young. Their parents did not teach them; sometimes the parents do not know any better, as they themselves were not taught these skills.

With many fathers, their easy way to deal with their insecurities around their families is through control and aggression. Some leave their responsibilities for their wives; they stay back and watch their wives fail or succeed. If she fails, she faces criticism from him; if she succeeds, the husband takes credit for her hard work. Some men who marry strong and capable women let their wives take full or most of the responsibility of running their homes. When a woman assumes the role of a man or of both man and woman in the house, the result is fatigue, tiredness, unhappiness, and poor health, because she has little or no time to take care of herself.

It would be wise for parents to teach their children, especially their male children, responsibilities so they can grow up as responsible adults.

In most African communities, boys are not taught to be responsible for anything, with few exceptions. Girls do the housework and cooking chores, while the boys play. When I was growing up, the girls in the family did almost every chore. Boys did almost nothing. Occasionally, they went to the farm with their father; other times, when they didn't feel like going, they stayed home.

I moved from a country where women are of less value, compared to Canada, where women are treated with respect, children are protected by law, and both male and female children are treated equally. Men's attitude in this culture is so different from that of African countries. Male children growing up in these societies have an idea of how to treat their women with love and respect and how to treat each other with respect, because that is what they see growing up with their fathers. Marriage in these cultures is by choice and with love between two adults who are committed to each other. These committed couples do things together, from housework to raising children. This is unlike most marriages in Africa, the Middle East, and Asia, where most men leave all the work for women; in some cases, even farm work is left for women.

Some African men who immigrate to the civilized world leave their financial responsibilities to their wives as well as the running of their homes. These men sit and watch their wives labor for their pleasure and do nothing. Some get married to professionals in order to enjoy their paychecks. Women are called "gold-diggers" when they marry men for money and not love, but there are more men who are gold-diggers in some cultures than women.

In forced marriages, everything is forced; sexual relationships with their wives are with force and not with love. In these cultures, not only are wives expected to do all the housework, they are also expected to be the best in bed. If the wife refuses sex because she's tired, she is beaten and forced;

in some cases, women are killed by their husbands for depriving them of what they call their "sexual rights."

What is surprising is that some men only exercise their power, authority, and control over women of their own culture. They easily change their attitudes when they marry women from other cultures.

Some African men who travel away from their countries and have the opportunity to date or marry foreign women (from a different race or culture than theirs) often condemn women from their own culture for not performing well in bed, the way foreigner women do. If African men are in relationships with foreign women (whether as lovers or wives), their attitude is completely different. Many treat their foreign women as gold. They do things for these foreign women that they would have never done for women from their own culture.

When these men are in relationships with foreign women, most of them do all the housework (grocery shopping, laundry, cleaning, and cooking). If men did what they do for foreign women with their African women, the women would prove them wrong in bed. Get real, men; this is a real world. You cannot have your cake and eat it too. A woman cannot be your slave in the day and perform as a queen in bed at night in a way to please you. Remember that you get what you put out. If you enslave your wife during the day, what you get is a tired and helpless wife at night. It is a woman's right to satisfy her husband in bed and give him her unconditional love, but the husband has to first love and treat her with respect. "It takes two to tangle." If your marriage is not going well, and you are not getting the satisfaction you expect from your wife, check yourself first. It may be what you are not doing right. Some of the above attitudes also stem from the lack of education of both the man and woman.

In a civilized word, education affects the behavior of people and the way men treat and respect women. In African countries, poverty and lack of education, especially for women, play an important role in the way boys, men, and fathers treat their women and in the way girls and women accept abuse from their husbands. In most African countries, some men still treat their wives as servants. When I talk about education, it does not only mean paper certificates or a degrees from a college or university. It also means common sense, good manners, and respect. Please don't get me wrong; I am not saying that education is not good. It is an important part of life, but education without common sense, good manners, and respect makes you no better than an illiterate. Remember that education didn't fall from the sky; it was started by people with wisdom, common sense, vision, and good thinking.

Some men are not fit physically or emotionally and are lacking the wisdom, maturity, patience, good manners, love, consideration, caring attitude, compromise, and self-control to be a good husband. If a young man wishes to get married and does not have what it takes to be a good husband, he needs to learn it before getting married. You can only be a good husband and a good father if you have most of these qualities. This also applies to women who wish their marriages to succeed.

So often you hear that parents are worried about their children not getting married at a certain age. What you do not often hear is a parent saying, "Does my son or daughter have all it takes to be a good and responsible husband or wife? Have I shown him or her love and taught him or her to love others?" Maturity does not come with age. Your son may be big and old enough, but if he is not wise, his age and size will not make him a good husband. A large kingdom and a big chair do not make a good king. What makes a good king is his wisdom. There are teenagers who are much more mature than fifty year old adults. Plus, the size of a man does not determine his strength and ability. Some people never grow up, even in wisdom. Certain manners have to be taught at home. As they say, "Charity begins at home." Some fathers wish for their children to grow in wisdom and be successful, but they refuse to contribute to their success. It is most likely that your children will end up like you or worse off, and your son may treat his wife the way you treat his mother. Men may take advantage of your daughter. As a father, you should take the lead and put your house in order.

Mothers are as important to children as fathers are. Do not exclude your wife or deny her right to parent your children with you. No one person should play the role of father and mother. Sons may be closer to their fathers and daughters to their mother at some point in life, but both need direction from both parents, especially from fathers in some countries. The way you live and do things before your son/daughter is the example they will follow. You are the mirror in which your children will see themselves. Fathers that treat their wives and children with respect are teaching them to treat other men and women with respect.

Show and provide for your children by your hard work, and they will learn to work hard and be responsible parents when they grow up. The excuse some fathers use when they fail to provide the basic necessities of life for their children is that they did not have the same opportunity with their fathers when growing up, so they don't think it is necessary to work extra hard to give their children what they did not have. Some may think that they did well, even with the little support from their parents, and they may think the little they got was all their children should have. That may be the standard of life that applied to them at the time, but things are different now. They should remember that their children need more than what they had in their day. Some fathers also claimed they were not in a good relationship with their fathers, so they do not know how to be a better role model in their children's lives.

Even if your relationship with your father was not the best, remember that what happened to you when you were growing up is not your children's fault. Your parents may have provided for you based on their standard of living at the time. You have the chance now to change things. Some behavior that was accepted in your parents' day is now regarded as a crime. Learn, if you have to, and stay close to your children. If you did not get the best lesson from your parents while growing up, you can learn from others or in school, and be a good example for your children, especially your sons. Your example will go a long way to prepare them for the better life you wish you had.

Always involve your wife in bringing up your children, as two heads are better than one. "You may not be able to do it alone, ask for wisdom from your wives" (Proverbs 23:24). Sometimes she knows more than you give her credit for, and remember that you can never be both father and mother. There is a good reason why God made her your wife.

Your wife can be your strength in your struggle to teach your children the right things. Your wife can be a good support when raising your children if she is given the opportunity to do her work as a mother. If you do not give her the chance and freedom to provide assistance to you, your children's future may be affected. You can never parent effectively without each other's assistance. It is a package that goes together well. It is very important to teach your children what they should know about marriage before they are old enough to marry.

As mentioned earlier, most forced marriages are initiated by fathers, and child abuse starts at home; in most cases, it also starts from the father. Most fathers control their wives and children and leave them with no voice; some neglect their role as husband and father. As stated in the Bible, "A father is to provide love, care, protection, shelter, food, clothing and security for his children until they are adults" (1 Timothy 8). When he forces his children to marry a stranger and to marry someone they do not love for his financial gain, he has failed his children in so many ways.

A father's position in the family is as the head and a provider. A father must be able to do the following for his children:

- Provide education
- Direct them
- Provide them with a solid foundation in which to build their lives

"Teach your child how he should live, and he will remember it all his life" (Proverbs 22:6).

A father must *not* do the following with regard to his children:

31

- He must not use them for financial reasons
- He must not enslave them
- He must not abuse them
- He must not neglect them

Some men blame their wives for their downfall, especially those that mistreat their wives and children and pray that it will be well with them. "You pray and ask why he no longer accepts them. It is because he knows you have broken your promise to the wife you married when you were young. She was your partner and you have broken your promise to her, although you promised before God, that you would be faithful to her. Didn't God make you one body and spirits with her? What was his purpose in this? It was that you should have children who are truly God's people. So make sure that none of you breaks his promise to his wife" (Malachi 2:14–16).

Some men suddenly decide to break their promises to their wives and marry another woman. Some excuses men give are:

- My wife is too old
- I travel a lot and can't take my wife with me
- I don't want to take my wife everywhere as I want her to stay home and look after our children
- My wife cannot give birth to male children
- My wife is not educated and cannot represent me in the public

Note that a man who married another woman for the reasons stated above does so against the word of God. "I tell you then, that any man who divorce his wife for any cause other than her unfaithfulness, commits adultery if he married another woman" (Matthew 19:19). In the eye of nonbelievers and their cultural beliefs, men in this culture do not believe in adultery, and some don't even know the meaning of the word adultery. They believe that it is a man's right to marry as many women as he can, and it's also a man's right to treat women the way he wants and divorce her when he wants.

God made a powerful statement with regard to this: "I hate it when one of you does such a cruel things to his wife." Malachi 2:14–16 clearly states that God does not take a casual view of marriages. He takes note of how husbands and wives treat each other. Therefore, a man should fulfill his duty as a husband, and a woman should fulfill her duty as a wife, and each should satisfy the other's needs. A wife is not the master of her own body, but her husband is; in the same way, a husband is not the master of his body but the wife is. "Men ought to love their wives just as they love their own bodies; A man who loves his wife loves himself" (Ephesians 5:28). "Marriage is to be honored by all, and husbands and wives must be faithful to each other" (Hebrews 13:4).

CHAPTER 6

Personal Experience

In my early years, growing up in the village, I observed many girls affected by arranged and forced marriages. Marriages that were secretly arranged by their parents affected both men and women, but young girls were mostly affected by this. I saw the pain and agony most of those girls went through. Some of them ended up heartbroken; there were suicide attempts and low self-esteem, and the majority of them ended up in polygamy, with abusive husbands, co-wife abuse, and sometimes abuse by the co-wives' older children. Only very few grew to love their husbands over time; many remained married and suffered in silence because they had no choice.

I will now take you through one of the stories that relates to forced marriages that my grandma told me, which shows that forced marriages does not only affect the person involved but some other members of the family. Even with strong evidence of cruelty in forced marriages, people still believe it is the best for their children.

The story of a girl (I'll call her Innocent) happened many years ago. Her father was a farmer, and her mom was a housewife. Both were well respected in the community. Innocent was born into a large family, but though she had lots of siblings, she grew up like an only child with her grandparents. She was very young when her grandparents took her in their care, with her parents' permission. Growing up, she thought her grandparents were her biological parents, and she referred to them as Mommy and Daddy.

Her grandparents were both hardworking and were very loved by many people around them. They raised her with love, and she always talked about their kindness and care of her.

My grandma said that Innocent, who grew to be a beautiful young girl, was like a grandchild to her because her parents were close family friends. One afternoon on village market day, which was every five days, Innocent was visiting with friends after school. It was the last day of school before the summer holiday. One of her cousins called her and told her that her grandma wanted her at home. She went home immediately. On getting home, she saw a lady talking with her grandma in the sitting room. She greeted her with familiarity because she had seen her couple of times during other visits to her parents. As she was about to go in to the room, her grandma called her back and told her that her father had asked the lady to return with her at the end of the market day.

Innocent was very happy to hear that she was going with her to visit with her parents and her siblings. She thought it was one of those holiday visits with her parents and others. She got very excited and did not ask any questions. She got ready at once, but something didn't seem right, for she saw sadness on her grandma's face; her grandma was almost in tears. She thought her mood was because she already was missing her. Innocent told her not to be sad and told her that she would only be away for couple of weeks, as usual, but her grandma knew better.

The day was getting dark, and market activities were over, and people were returning to their different destinations. The lady told her grandma that it was time to go back. She said if it became any later than that, they would not be able to get transport back. Her grandma prayed for their safe journey back home and then escorted them outside to wait for a truck. On market days at that time, trucks were mostly use to transport people and their goods to and from different villages and cities.

It took about three hours to get a truck that had enough space for both of them. The journey took a couple of hours because of bad roads and due to the truck driver dropping off other people and their goods along the way. It takes a lot less time to travel to the villages these days because the roads are a lot better, and transportation is more modern. People no longer travel in those trucks; they are now used only for transporting goods.

Five days into Innocent's visit, she was out playing with friends and her older sister when her father sent for them to come home. When they got there, she saw some people visiting with her father in the living room. Her older sister was about sixteen years old at the time. To her great surprise, she found out that the visitors were there to take her sister to her future father–in–law's house. They had arranged to take her to her husband, who lived in a big city far away from the village. This type of arrangement was common then and still is now in some villages. Both Innocent and her sister knew nothing about this arrangement or about the husband.

The traditional marriage was arranged so secretly that none of them knew anything about it until her sister was taken to her husband. Innocent's father asked Innocent's sister to get ready and was told she was leaving with the visitors right away. They could not believe what they were hearing and could not believe that their father could ever arrange for her sister's marriage when she was so young. Her sister's dream of going to high school and doing things other young girls took for granted was shattered before her eyes. Upon hearing this, her sister started crying hysterically, begging their father not to let her go. Her voice was so loud that it was heard throughout the streets as she repeatedly begged their father, "Don't do this to me. Father, please let me stay." Her cries fell on deaf ears. They had no mercy for her, and nobody listened to her cry.

Her mom went into the kitchen with tears in her eyes. When something like this happens, mothers feel the pain of their children. Their mom probably did not wish her daughter to go through that, but she could not do anything to stop it. In those days, women had no say or right in their husband's house; whatever the husband decided for the family is what they did. Even if women wanted to protect their children and provide them with better lives, they could not do so because they were under the control of their husbands. They were helpless and only watched their children go in the direction chosen for them by their fathers. When such children grow up, they also remain under the control of their husbands. Innocent's sister tried to run away but was stopped by some of her cousins who were standing and watching. Even in her sister's agony, the visitors told her sister to stop crying and to pack her stuff, while their father sat entertaining the visitors as if nothing was wrong. It was so sad and painful to watch her cry so much. She refused to pack her stuff, but regardless of whether she packed her stuff or not, they planned to take her away, with or without any belongings.

While they were still crying, their father called Innocent and asked her to pack her stuff as well because she would be going with her sister as an escort to her husband's house. She would come back when her sister was fully settled into her husband's house. He did not tell them how many days, weeks, months, or years before she would return. Both girls were overwhelmed with everything that was happening that they could not ask any questions.

Back in those days (I think it is still happening in most communities in Africa) it was very important that someone go with a new wife to her husband's home to spend time with her until she was comfortable in her husband's house. In some cultures, an elderly woman goes with her, but in other cultures, a younger person goes with her, and it is always someone in the family. The person goes with her to give her the necessary support and then returns after a while or stays with her as long as she wants, if the father wishes for her to stay.

Innocent's sorrow doubled and her pain increased as well. She wanted to turn to her mom for help and protection, but it was obvious that her mother needed help too. Mothers are supposed to protect their children, but most times, women are physically and emotionally damaged themselves and cannot help their own children.

Just like her sister, Innocent did not want to go, but she did not have a choice; she had to obey their father. Her mother helped her to put her belongings together, and as soon as she was done packing, she heard one of the men call out, "Let's go. It's getting late." They had a car in front of their house so they did not have to walk far. They went in the car, crying as they waved goodbye to everyone. People, in turn, waved and watched in horror as they were driven away by the strangers.

Innocent's sister was put in the middle seat of the car, with one men on each side of her. Innocent sat in the front seat with the driver. In some cases, a forced marriage felt like being kidnapped. There was no ceremony, not even the traditional one for Innocent's sister. From the moment she knew about her sister's secret forced marriage, Innocent suspected that some day she might be forced to marry a total stranger in just the same way, without any kind of ceremony. This thought was scary.

The marriage ceremony should be a happy moment for both groom and bride. When this is lacking, the joy and the spirits of marriage is incomplete.

Forced Marriages Are Not Ceremonial

Normal marriage, whether it is white wedding or traditional wedding, is always a big occasion. It is a way to say goodbye to single life and welcome to married life. This is also a ceremony for the family of the man and woman to let everyone know that their son or daughter is leaving their father and mother to live together and become one.

In forced marriages, there is no ceremony of any kind. Most traditional African marriages, except in the case of forced marriages, are always followed by celebrations. Traditional marriages do not require that the couple attend church services or wear white gowns. The couples are usually dressed in traditional attire; this type of ceremony is usually done in three stages in most Nigerian culture. Some might be slightly different from the other, but it is the same idea. Below is the sequence in which traditional marriages take place in most Nigerian cultures under normal circumstances.

(1) The introduction: In a normal traditional marriage, introduction plays a very important role, leading to most successful marriages. This is a formal introduction, where the man introduces his girlfriend to his parents; also, the girl introduces her boyfriend to her parents. The initial introduction can be just the boy and girl. This is usually done without a crowd, most times with just the two of them or with the company of a couple of friends. Both make their intentions to marry each other known to their parents. If both parents agree for them to marry, a day would then be set for the two parents to met and talk about their children's plans. Both sets of parents bring a few elder members of their families. At this meeting, the father of the groom officially asks the girl's parents for the girl's hand in marriage to his son.

The parents of the girl then ask their daughter if she is serious about her intention to marry the boy. The answer is always yes. Other than that question, the boy and girl play little or no role at this meeting. They watch and listen. From this day onward, their relationship will be recognized. Both the boy and girl are well known to both parents now. After this, a day is set for an official introduction meeting that usually involves other members and friends of both families. In most cultures, the parents of the groom take the lead to arrange and finance the introduction meeting. After this meeting, the fathers of the boy and the girl would send messages to their family members about their children's plan to get married, and they extend invitations for the official traditional marriage ceremony that will follow. The wedding may be a big ceremony, with dances and native songs and may involve cultural dances or live band music, depending on the wealth of the families.

(2) The second stage of the ceremony is when the girl's father calls the members of his family and tells them about his intention to give his daughter's hand in marriage. He informs them of the date for the dowry and of the big ceremony.

(3) The third step is the actual ceremony. On this day, the husband-to-be and his family come to the bride's house with everything needed for the ceremony; cola-nut, pine-wine, palm-oil, yams, dried fish, beverages, alcohol, and other things required per individual culture and traditional beliefs. These items are assembled and presented to the girl's father, in the presence of his family. The future groom and bride are present, as their presence is very important on this day.

At this ceremony, the boy and girl are well dressed in African attire. The parents and elder members of the girl's family ask their daughter over and over if she is ready to marry the boy and if she wants them to accept the gifts. Her answer is very important, as their acceptance or rejection of the items depends on her answer; she answers yes. I have not seen any girl say no on this day; it would only happen in the case of forced marriages; but then this type of ceremony would not take place. In some cultures, a cup filled with pine-wine is given to the girl to give to her boyfriend, who is sitting among his family members. This is for the girl to identify her boyfriend and to show everyone present that she knows who the husband-to-be is. Once she identifies him by giving him the wine, both the boy and girl drink from the same cup of wine. This is a way for the girl to tell his father and other family members that it is okay for them to accept the gift.

As soon as the girl's father gets the okay from his daughter to accept the gift, he announces his daughter's acceptance to his family members. Even though they have observed this ceremony, it is a traditional right for the girl's father to confirm and clarify things for them. Once this is done, the boy and the girl are pronounced husband and wife. The new couples are escorted to the dance floor by their parents and then later join by members of the high table, which consist of the elders in the family. In the absence of elderly family members, other close family friends (elders) can represent them. From then on, the bride and groom are basically on the dance floor, dancing all night, as long as the party lasts, except for meal breaks and time out to change their outfits. This is the time when bride and groom dress their best and show everyone what they can afford. Those who can't afford expensive clothes will rent clothing. Family members, friends, and well-wishers will dance with the couple wearing different colored uniforms. This is a way some people also show their support to the bride and groom, as these uniforms are purchased from the bride at a high price. Sometimes they pay more than double the price the bride paid. The costs of the uniforms depend on the social class of the bride and groom. If the bride and groom are from rich families, the uniform can be very expensive, which means a higher profit for the bride and groom.

While some dance to music, others socialize with each other. In most cultures, people do not necessarily buy gifts. They show their support by spraying (putting money) on the couple's heads while they dance; the money replaces the gift. They are no limits on how much a person can spray; it depends on the individuals and the social class of people. The money they collect at the end of the ceremony is given to the bride and groom for their personal use. From that day on, they are both recognized as "husband and wife" and are addressed as such. A special day is set for the family members to escort the girl into the husband's house. It can be the husband's family house or his own house, based on her husband's arrangements.

As for Innocent and her sister, the journey to the father-in-law's house was three villages away from their father's village. It was a very quiet trip; the men were chatting and making jokes. They tried to make the girls happy and tried to tell her sister the positive things about marriage, what to do, what to expect, and how to respond to her husband and others. They tried very hard to give her the advice her father and mother should have given her.

When they reached her sister's father-in-law's house, there were lots of people waiting for their arrival. The people were drinking, eating, and celebrating a new "wife" to their family. Some of them got up to greet her sister, but she never answered them. She pushed them away and continued to cry hysterically. They offered her a seat, but she refused to sit down. A few minutes later, she was taken to her room, which she shared with Innocent until arrangements were made by her father-in-law to take her to her husband in the city.

The unfortunate thing was that her arranged husband did not even know her. He was only aware that his father had arranged a wife for him and was probably told her name and maybe a little description of her and her family history. Innocent's sister found out that she was her husband's third wife; he had married twice and divorced one of them some years back.

Shattered Dream

Girls have so many wishes and dreams while growing up. Getting married, having a big wedding, and being escorted by her father to her husband on the day of her wedding is one of a girl's biggest dreams. A girl's hope is to marry a young, responsible, loving, and caring husband who will share experiences with her. As a little girl, I used to play boyfriend/girlfriend or husband/wife with my friends. The boys automatically assumed the role of fathers, and the girls assumed the role of mothers without thinking.

On her wedding day, the girl's father shows his high respect and love to her before he proudly gives her hand in marriage to her husband and wishes her good luck and farewell; this ceremony is always emotionally and joyfully performed. The father rests his responsibility of caring for his daughter, including financial responsibilities, in the hands of his daughter's husband. Before this ceremony, he would have performed his duty as a good father, caring for and providing education for his daughter.

A girl's relationship with her father means so much. Girls look up to their fathers for so many things; not just material things, but also for love and security. In most civilized societies, the bond between father and daughter starts from the day she is born. Daughters have a better relationship with their fathers at an early age, until they reach puberty. After puberty, fathers pull back a little. There is still love and caring between them, but fathers keep a bit of distance at this age and involve the mothers more in the daughters' lives. A little bit of awkwardness comes with puberty for girls, and fathers are not too comfortable dealing with that and may not know the right approach.

Like most children, Innocent's sister had a dream of what she wanted to do when she grew up, but her dream was shattered the day she was forced to her husband's house. One of her dreams was to attend a higher institution after finishing grade six. Education was her first priority at the time. She planned to attend what was then Modern School with some of her friends. When her father did not give a favorable answer when she asked him to pay her school fees, she asked some schoolteachers to plead with her father on her behalf. The teachers went to her father on her behalf to sponsor her to a higher institution. As they put it. She was a very brilliant and clever girl. They pleaded and begged on her behalf for her father to give her the opportunity to get an education.

She was hopeful that her father would change his mind about allowing her to attend, but she did not know that her father had another plan for her. Her father never said no to her request, but he used every delay and excuse on why she should wait.

Innocent's sister was never given the chance to get an education, which she could have used as a weapon to say no to the forced marriage. In today's society, many women are educated and are brave and able to say no when things do not seem right for them. Many are reaching out for help and finding their way out of unhealthy relationships, including forced marriages, bad relationships with an arranged husband, or dealing with co-wives. They are able to access resources that help to overcome their fear and increase their self-esteem.

Some girls are forced to marry at a most vulnerable age; just like Innocent's sister. What her sister needed at the time was an education, love, direction, support, and care from her parents; not a husband and not to be a wife at age sixteen. She was robbed of her youth when she was forced to marry a stranger at that age. She never knew what it felt like to be a youth or teenager, growing up with her parents. She went from being a child to being a wife, and worst of all, she was forced into polygamy. She never knew what it's like to be in love or to be loved. She grew up as a restricted teenager in her husband's house, instead of a happy girl in her father's house. She never had the time to do what girls do at her age; for example, get an education, guidance from her parents, and freedom to choose her own husband. Like many girls forced to marry, the experience was devastating. When this happens, separation from their families and the isolation of being in new places affects their confidence level and their self-esteem.

Every child needs love, care, and support from their parents. If a girl is forced to marry at the time when she most needs her parents, at a developing stage of a girl's life, and especially when she marries into polygamy or marries a man old enough to be her father, she misses the chance to grow up with the important people in her family. What hurts even more in the forced marriages is that the girls often are not given the chance to say a proper goodbye to their loved ones and do not have the chance to experience their youth. When those days are gone, they can never be relived; they were robbed of their youth. It is also painful that the community watched as these children suffered some of the following, which is associated with forced marriage:

- Depression
- Insecurity
- Emptiness
- Lack of freedom
- Low self esteem

After staying in her father-in-law's house for about two months, he then decided it was time to send her to join her husband in city. Her grandfather and grandma were there the night before she left for the city to wish her well and to say goodbye. She did not really pay much attention to them because they had supported her forced marriage. It was not so much her grandma; women had no say in their husband's house at the time, but it was hard not to include her in it. Grandma tried to give motherly advice, but it was too late. She was too upset to listen to anything Grandma or Grandpa had to say.

It was very early in the morning when her father-in-law's wife woke up Innocent and her sister to get ready for the city. Her sister started crying again. They were offered breakfast, but her sister refused. Innocent ate a little because she was very hungry. After they showered, they were escorted into a waiting car. The driver had been sent from the city by her husband. Though neither of them wanted to go to the city under the circumstances, they were both relieved to know that they were not going by public transportation, which would have taken at least a couple of days; the journey to city then was always long because of the bad roads, and drivers stopped to pick up other passengers on the way. But with private transport, there were no delays; even then, it usually took a whole day to get to the city.

The driver stopped twice on the way for meals. Innocent ate the two times, but her sister only ate a little once. The trip was very quiet because the driver did not know them to carry on a long conversation. The fact that her sister was crying did not help. Innocent fell asleep a few times, and each time she woke up, her sister was still crying. When they got to the city, Innocent was excited to see the big tall buildings and the reflection of lights everywhere. It was unlike the village, which was always dark at night. She thought this was not bad after all, but she did not know about anything else. It took about fourty five minutes from the time they arrived in the city to reach the husband's house.

When they got there, Innocent's sister met her husband for the very first time. She was shocked at his age, but there was nothing she could have done about it. Her husband received them very well; he appeared very excited and happy to see his new wife. He lived in a very big two-story building, with so many rooms that there was enough room for her sister and the other wife, his children, and house helpers. He appeared a genuinely nice person. He did his very best to make them happy, especially for the first few weeks, but her sister was very unhappy.

After a while Innocent's sister accepted that "what cannot be changed can be endured." She started opening up and learning to be a wife. Her husband was a very kind man; he was a father figure, as in reality, he was old enough to be their father. Right from the day they arrived in the city, Innocent started calling him Daddy. He displayed every quality of a good father.

Innocent's sister went to his house with little clothing and belongings. Remember that she was not at all ready for marriage at that age. Her mom and grandma had wanted to buy her some clothing when she was in the father-in-law's house, but the father-in-law discouraged them and told them that his son would take care of everything. A week or so after arriving at her husband's house, he gave her money to do her personal shopping, including household items, and his driver took them shopping. He had just been transferred to this city and had not fully settled in. His other wife and his children were still in the other state, waiting for him to send for them.

9

Mixed Marriage

I nnocent's sister struggled to adjust to a stranger, now her husband. She had to because she did not have a choice. It was so obvious that there was no romance in the relationship. It was not like a young man and young woman's relationship, and it was kind of awkward because of the age difference. It was like a father and daughter relationship, but it was different because she was expected to play the role of a wife in every aspect, without experience in anything. He had all the experience and maturity of a father and a husband. He tried very hard to show her his "divided love"; I call it divided love because he was also married to another woman. Any man who is married to more than one wife does not have unconditional love; in some cases, he is not truthful to his wives. His feelings for his wives are not real. He might favor one to the other. He may be kind and patient, but that does not change his ability to offer unconditional love.

Innocence's sister was emotionally scarred; this could be traced back to the time she was taken by force to marry a stranger. Her dream ended before it even started.

About six or nine months after they arrived in the city, her husband sent for his other wife and children. Not long after the arrival of his family, fights started between Innocent's sister and the co-wife. There was fighting over one thing or another, sometimes over the smallest things. It was like watching children fighting over toys' because of her age and under the circumstances that led to her marriage. She did very well as a young wife, defending herself whenever there was a fight. She had to do so because she had no father or mother to turn to at her rough times.

The only father she had and needed was God. She realized there was no help from anyone else but God during her struggle. She then started going to church, where she made some friends of her age. Some were married and some were not; she was able to relate to them in so many ways, which made her a little happy and made her realize that she was not the only one in her situation. There were a few members in her church with the same problem (forced to marry at a young age and some into polygamy), and they all were trying to survive.

After a year of staying in the city with her sister, Innocent had to go back to her grandpa and grandma. It took her quite a while to get used to village life again, but gradually she adjusted. Innocent was a bit happy, knowing that her sister was a bit happier and closer to God. Some young women who find themselves in this situation barely survive; some of them do not survive at all.

10

Story Time

T hat was the end of the story Grandma told me; but I had questions after the story time. Grandma answered them as clearly as she could.

"Why didn't Innocent's sister run away to escape the forced marriage?", I asked.

"She probably wanted to, but in her case, there was nowhere to run, and no one would listen.", grandma replied.

"How can a mother let her child suffer like that and do nothing to help her?", I asked.

"Some mothers are physically, mentally, and emotionally damaged themselves, to the point where they cannot help themselves or their children.", Grandma replied.

I then asked my grandma how she knew this story like it was her own. She said it was because Innocent's parents and her family were very close friends. Grandma and Innocent's mother grew up in the same community and were from the same village. They told each other everything; there were no secrets between them. And when Innocent returned to the village, she provided all the details of her journey.

"Grandma, why did Innocent's mother not at least say something or do something to help her daughter?", I asked.

"She did not refuse to help Innocent's sister; she was helpless and couldn't help her. When you grow up, you will understand what I am talking about.", grandma replied.

"Explain to me now, Grandma; maybe I will understand.", I said.

"My child, it is hard for a woman who has not given birth to explain birth labor. You cannot understand it now.", grandma replied.

"But you are always speaking in parables. This makes it even harder to understand your explanation.", I said.

"What an elderly person experiences over many years is hard to explain to a child in one story; again, my child, time will tell.", grandma replied.

"Grandma, why did no one, not even the girl's brother, do anything to help her if her mother was helpless? And why do men control their wives?", I asked.

"I cannot speak for all men, but the unfortunate thing is that this is a societal norm. When the young men grow up to be adult men in this society, they behave like their fathers because they follow the behavior modeled to them by their fathers. Have you heard the saying that the apple does not fall far from the tree? Well, it is for the same reason that girls behave like their mothers.", grandma replied.

"Was it a happy marriage for Innocent's sister?", I asked.

Grandma shook her head sadly. "Not really. After a long struggle, she finally got the courage and left, but could not leave with her children.", grandma replied.

"What then happened to her children?", I asked.

"Their father and their stepmother raised them, and they all turned out to be responsible and educated adults.", grandma replied.

"Grandma, how do I know for sure that what happened to Innocent's sister will not happen to me when I grow up?", I asked.

"I cannot say what will happen to you when you grow up; it will be your parents' decision.", grandma replied.

"Grandma, what happened to Innocent herself? Was her marriage also forced?", I asked.

Grandma smiled and said, "Innocent moved back to the city, after completing her primary school education, to join her sister. She found a man, brought the man home to introduce him to her parents, and her parents approved of him. They did the traditional marriage for them, and then they went back to the city and performed the white wedding."

Innocent's sister's story may seem like something from the past, but similar situations still occur in most African societies today. In fact, I narrowly escaped an arranged forced marriage myself. I managed to abort it, in part because of some of the stories Grandma told me and because I saw other girls being pushed into marriage by their parents.

Storytelling and story time in the village was not just about telling stories; it was a way of socializing with each other and grandparents having fun with their grandchildren and getting to know them better. It was also the way of sharing wisdom. But storytelling was not peculiar to grandparents; parents and others told stories too, but they were always something special about grandparents' stories.

When it was story time, the elders sometimes joined us when we socialized in the moonlight and told us stories of their past or stories told to them by their elders. Everyone sat on the floor in a circle, and the elder or elders sat on a stool, or sometimes they sat on the floor as well. Some other times, it was just me and couple of my friend with my grandma and grandpa. My grandpa would sometimes sit on his handmade woven rocking chair while telling his stories. The chair was the best; if Grandpa left the chair for a moment, we would all rush to the chair and sometimes fight over who sat there. Looking back, it was a wonderful time we children spent with grandparents.

Story time releases stress for people, and it's a good way to end the day. It was another way the community got together to create fun and laughter. It also made life less complicated for them.

CHAPTER 11

Back from the City

I had the opportunity to leave the village for about a year before I finished primary school, and I stayed with one of my aunties who had been forced to marry her husband at a young age. My visit with her was supposed to be for a short time, but my grandparents gave me permission to extend my stay with her for about a year, because she struggled for a while to fit into her new role as a wife in her early marriage.

After staying for such a long time in the city, the city kind of got the village life out of me, and I almost didn't want to go back. While in the city, I noticed that city girls had more opportunities and freedom than the girls in the village, but I had to go back to my grandparents.

The first few months back to the village were really hard, because I knew then the difference between village living and living in the city. It was like returning from light to dark. There was electricity in the city, as well as TV and other conveniences that were lacking in the village. It took me some time to get used to it again. It was nice to see my grandparents, but I really missed city living.

Getting used to village life again was a bit of a challenge. There are more advantages to living in the village than living in the city. Some of these advantages include growing up in a tight-knit family. Families are very close with each other, and they do things together as families. They interact well with each other. The beauty of it all is that everything is natural, from the food you eat to the air you breathe. There are no chemicals; everything is homemade and without preservatives. Though there were lots of conveniences in the city, the villagers made provisions when possible.

There was no electricity in the villages then, but now some villages have electricity. They made use of the sun and moonlight (God-given light). There was no tap water, but they substituted it with fresh river water or rain (chemical-free). People were content with what they had and what they could afford. The stress rate was far less than it was in the city. People did not compete over material things.

There is family unity in the village. People care for one another and show their love to each other. Everyone knows each other and shows concern for each other. The children play freely together, as if they are of the same parents; parents show love and concern about other children and not only their own children. The saying that "it takes a village to raise a child" stands out very much in the village.

People sleep better because nights are quieter. There is no night duty or shift work, only farm work and petty trading. Everything people do is finished before dark. There isn't much sound to distract people, only if there is an emergency. In case of emergencies, the elders and adults in the village wake up to help each other out and support each other through whatever the problems are.

You hardly hear the sound of cars, motorcycles, or other noisy objects at night. People are energetic in the morning because they've had a good night's sleep; they get up early to face the day's challenges, and whatever is not done before dark can only be done the next day; there isn't much people can do after sundown without electricity. The villagers depend on the use of lanterns at night, which does not offer much bright light; just enough to see a very short distance. It is not bright enough to use for major work that requires brighter light.

The crime rate in the village is almost zero percent because everyone knows each other too well. Before people commit a crime, they would think of the negative impact it would have on them and the humiliation it would bring to their families if they were caught. Parents in some societies are held responsible for crimes committed by their children. For that reason, children avoid crime so they don't put their parents in trouble. The accident rate of any kind is far less in the village because people are more careful in what they do. Neighbors take turns volunteering to baby-sit each other's children so they don't have to pay for babysitting services.

Everyone socializes happily together most times. No one is by himself. The poor are not left out of activities or social gatherings. The gap between the poor and the rich is not very wide. There is a great feeling of freedom in the village; freedom of speech, freedom of movement, jokes and laughter. There are more happy times in the village than in the city. Family and neighbor relationships are very close.

In the city, people do not have time for each other due to the busy lifestyles. Everyone seems to be in a hurry all the time. Some do not even have time for their children. In most areas in the city, you do not even know who your neighbors are, and people sleepless, work more, and spend less time socializing. People are always running to go to work and back as if they are pursued by a wild animal. Children spend less quality time with their parents; some children hardly see their parents, as most parents jump from one job to another to pay for the conveniences in the home. There is peace of mind, and people are more forgiving in the village than in the city. People in the city are less relaxed, as they always worry about work and other things. Village lifestyle is very inclusive and more relaxed, and people are more content, friendly, and more welcoming. The environment is also welcoming. Everyone socializes freely with each other.

People in the village are very nice to each other. Most of them have good hearts. They may not go to church regularly, but many of them are good in sharing with others. As stated in Roman 12:13: "Share your belonging with your needy people fellow Christian, and open your home to stranger." In the village, for example, if a visitor came to your next-door neighbor but the neighbor wasn't at home, you would take the visitor into your home, offer him food, and make him feel welcome until your neighbor returned, even if it meant keeping him in your home for longer than a day. This could occur if your neighbor did not return the same day, and the visitor came from a distance away because transportation was not frequent in the villages in those days. It's all different now; but back then, there were no hotels or motels. In those days, unless visitors gave advance notice through market people, there was a chance that their hosts would not meet the guest at home, especially if it was farm season. There were no telephone services in the villages in those days, but now there are cell phones. Emergency visits would mean you were taking chances.

When I first returned from the city, people told me that I was distancing myself from friends and family members. This was unintentional; what I was doing was having some time for myself, as the crowd was overwhelming at times. I needed some time for myself. People would come to our house without notice; sometimes as many as five or more. This became strange to me because in the city, people would give notice before they visited, and the visits were not so frequent.

I think the reason the villagers do not give notice is because they know that you are always at home at a certain times of the day; they are right because there are not many places to go in the village, especially in the late hours. Some friends joked with me, saying, "You are now acting like a city girl." I apologized each time the jokes were made because I didn't mean to act any different from the other girls, but I think living in the city for a while got the village lifestyle out of me. Gradually, I changed my ways and became more of who I was before I left for the city.

In the city, people are very private and closed-off. They mind their business and are less sociable and less welcoming, which in a way is good; but it makes people look cold on the outside. In the village, people are more open; sometimes too open, to the point of no privacy. The disadvantage of this is that most villagers are noisy and do not mind their business. You can hardly do things in the village without people knowing or commenting on it. There is no privacy in the village; people socialize outside a lot; from eating outside to talking. They talk about anything and anyone; both positive and negative, and at times stories about people are repeated over and over. You feel sometimes that you are living in the public eye, where people know your every move. This is not so in the city. Everything has advantages and disadvantages. You win some, and you lose some. You cannot have it all.

The amazing thing about the village is how people care and share things with each other; there were none of the modern conveniences or gadgets in the village when I was growing up. The only convenience we had was the radio, which was not affordable to everyone. People who could afford it shared with others. In the evening after dinner, those who did not have a radio would go to the homes of those people who had a radio and listen to music and to the news for couple of hours or so. It was rarely longer than a couple of hours because the batteries would need to be charged or replaced after that for the next day. In some cases, people shared the cost of replacing the radio batteries when needed. After listening to music and news from the city in the evening, we sometimes felt like we were a part of the city. It was always a joy to share the city news the next day with friends who did not have the opportunity to listen to radio. It was mostly good news from the city then, but that is all different today. There is more bad news from the city these days than good news, due to the extreme population increase in the city.

People are moving to the cities from the villages and other neighboring countries, seeking better lives. Some brought crime with them, and others took to a life of crime in the cities if they could not get what they hoped for and felt it was a shame returning home without achievements.

The same thing applied to the TV. For example, if one or two people had a TV, people gathered in their houses. If there were not enough seats in the TV room, people stood outside by the window and watched. Those who had TV and radio in the village were considered rich; they were always kind to share with the poor. Again, the TV was only watched for a couple of hours in the evening.

In the absence of TV or radio, people socialized with each other outside, told stories, and created activities that involved everyone who was interested in participating. There were no official social clubs or big restaurants to distract the social gathering or activities. There were a couple of local food canteens that closed as early as seven in the evening each day. Big occasions, like Easter, Christmas, Igue, and yam festivals were also celebrated in groups. There were lots to eat and drink, especially for children, in these celebrations. Most of these activities and celebrations did not involve a lot of money, as people shared and did potluck. People were very good in helping one another, and the "haves" shared with "have-nots." Social classes were not so noticeable, and no one was excluded from any activities or celebrations.

Most of these activities were community events and were held outdoors. They were always colorful; this is where people showed off their beautiful attire that they did not have time to show off when they were busy with farm work. Though there were no dress codes in these celebrations, people dressed in their best and in traditional attire. The food was always nice and fresh.

The city diet was also different. People would buy food and store it in the refrigerator for days before they ate it or before they used it. Lots of the food contained preservatives.

In the village, we basically ate what we grew in the farm, and it was always fresh; sometimes between what we grew in the farm and the sale of bush meat, my grandpa hunted. We always had much to eat; there was never food shortage, but other material things were not always at our disposal. Sometimes we sold food stuff to buy other things that were necessary and important.

Even without the big appliances and other leisure items, it was fun growing up in the village. Looking back, I did not really miss those material things that people took for granted in the city because it was just not one of the dreams in the village. And as they say, "You really don't miss what you don't have." We spent valuable time socializing in the moonlight instead of under electric lights.

Life has since improved in the village, as there is electricity now, but there are still more choices of everything and more opportunity in the city, especially for girls. All the same, I am blessed to have experienced both lifestyles.

CHAPTER 12

My Plan to Go Back to the City

From the day I returned from the city, I planned and dreamed to move back to the city for a better life and because I didn't want to be married to a stranger at a young age. To dream is one thing, but to make that dream a reality is another. I didn't know how to make my dream come true on my own, so I sought the help of a friend who also had the same dream, even though neither of us had any idea how to live our dreams. I had quite a few friends, but I trusted one more than the others; she became my best friend. She was a very good and reliable friend, and she was also my cousin. We both agreed to work on our dreams together, one person at a time.

Both my friend and I came up with this brilliant idea of saving money secretly for a rainy day. Our plan was to run away some day if our parents refused to send us to a higher institution after finishing primary school or if they arranged to marry us to strangers. We both started saving in cigarette cans that we used as piggy banks. We each had our own. In those days in the villages, there were no fancy plastic or ceramic piggy banks; there were only cans and bottles. We chose cans because they didn't break.

One day, a couple of years after my return to the village (I think I was in fifth grade) I was returning from school with my friend. She wanted to stop by my house and spend some time with me as her parents had gone to the farm, and she didn't want to be home alone. As we got close to my house, we noticed four cars parked in front of the house. I recognized one of the vehicles as belonging to one of our neighbor's sons, who lived in the city. He occasionally visited with his family in the village. When we got into the house, we noticed a large gathering in my grandpa's living room. We wanted to go in through the back door to avoid the crowd, but the back door was locked, so we had no choice but to go in through the front entrance, which meant we had to pass all the strangers in the living room.

At first I thought they were having one of their family meetings, which they held once a year. During that time my grandpa's families came from the city. Strangely, none of my grandpa's family from the city was there, but two of his brothers from the same village were at the meeting.

As we walked past the crowd, we greeted everyone with our knee bent, which was a sign of respect. If you don't do this when greeting your elders, you are considered disrespectful. In some other cultures in Nigeria, people greet their elders with their knees touching the ground; this has not changed.

As we walked through the crowd, I heard one of them say to the person sitting next to him, "She is beautiful." He pointed his finger toward me and added, "The one with the low cut." We did not stop to ask any questions; we walked past as if we did not hear what was said. We both went out the back door and to another friend's house and spent some time there. I could not stop wondering what was going on in our house and what the man's statement meant.

It was getting dark, and my friend had to go home. I needed to go home too because we did not have much to eat after school; we were both hungry. When I got home, the meeting was over, and everyone had left. I ate dinner, which Grandma saved for me. After eating, I sat quietly in the living room and did not say a word to my grandma. Grandma asked why I was so quiet. At first, I said nothing, but when she insisted that I tell her, I started crying and told her that I had a feeling that the meeting they had earlier was about me because I overhead what one of the men said about me. Grandma tried to hide the truth from me at first, but she later told me in secret that it was about my arranged marriage to the neighbor's son.

63

"The neighbor's son?", I cried out. "Grandma, you mean the one with the blue Peugeot car? The old man with the wife and children in the city?". I described him in every negative way I could. Right there, I assured my grandma that it never would happen. I repeatedly said, "Over my dead body, Grandma! It is never going to happen!" Grandma begged me not to let Grandpa know that she told me because it was supposed to be top secret until they thought I was ready to be kidnapped and shipped to the man's house.

When I thought of the man who was supposed to become my husband, I said to myself, "It is better I die than to marry that man". I wondered how my grandpa thought I could marry that man, especially with what I observed with some other girls in the village. I told myself that when the time came, Grandpa could kill me if he wanted, but I would never marry the man. I kept quiet because I did not want Grandpa to know that I knew what had happened. I did not want him to hate me, and I feared that if he knew that I knew, he might hasten his plan to send me to the man. I could not turn to my biological parents for help because I knew they were part of the plan.

From that day on, until I left the village, I became a different person, both at home and in school. I did not know the meaning of depression then, but knowing what I know now and thinking back at what I went through, I think I was suffering from some form of depression. I did not ask my grandpa about the meeting or let him know that Grandma told me anything, but my attitude toward my grandpa suddenly changed, and I could not hide it from him. Grandpa knew that I was not acting like myself but he didn't connect it to the meeting. I became very distant and secretive about almost everything. I was not the same happy girl he knew.

I overhead him one day telling Grandma how I had changed toward him, and he wondered why I had not changed toward my grandma. Grandma asked him, "Could it be that your approach has changed toward her?" Grandma knew the real reason but did not tell him. He concluded by saying that it was natural for a girl to be closer to women.

I was still very respectful toward him, but I did not trust him anymore. He was such a wonderful grandpa to me in every way until that incident. The incident was kind of sad; it was not something I forgot in a hurry, as it could have changed my life for the worst.

In school, I started withdrawing from friends and kept to myself a lot. My school grades were affected. Our head mistress asked me to a private meeting one day. She asked why my grades were dropping and if there was anything she could do to help. I told her there was nothing wrong and promised her that I would try my best to bring my grades up, which I did. I feared that if I told her what I was going through, she would tell my grandma and grandpa, and that would have put Grandma in big trouble. Things I use to share with friends about my grandma and grandpa became private because I was not happy with Grandpa, so I had nothing positive to say about him, and I did not want to only talk about Grandma. Instead, I stopped talking about both of them altogether.

I felt some other girls in school were luckier than I was because their parents did not arrange their marriages to total strangers at that age. I felt inferior to my friends, and at the same time, I thought there was no point in keeping friends when I knew that the relationships would not last due to the secret arranged marriage. I had one year left of school, and after the one year, there were a couple of things that would probably happen to me: either my grandpa would force me to marry the strange man, or I would commit suicide or run away. Regardless, I would lose all my friends. In my mind, there was no need to hold on to things I could not keep, and if anything happened to me, they would not miss me too much.

The only friend I could not stay away from was my best friend; she knew everything about me and was able to keep it a secret. She understood because her father had arranged and forced her brother to marrying a girl few years back, and according to her, the marriage was unsuccessful. She had the same fear that someday her father would arrange her marriage and force her to also marry. She was more focused in school; she was not directly affected. Instead of my concentrating on my homework after school, my mind was always occupied with thoughts of how I would escape from the village and where I was going if I did escape. The thoughts blocked my concentration at school. Even in the middle of playing with friends, the thought would come over me and sadness would follow. I sometimes excused myself and went home. I worried about my decision to run away and what would happen if it didn't work out. On the other hand, I thought it was a good decision, and I had to work hard to make it work because nothing was worse than forced marriage.

I continued to save. I usually didn't keep secrets from Grandma, but running away was a secret I had to keep. If she knew, she would tell my grandpa. On the last day of school, everyone was so happy about completing their primary school education. I was unhappy; I cried the whole day. I knew if I remained in the village, it would be the end of my education. My grandma asked if I failed my grades because it was unusual for a child to cry so much after school ended. The following day, my grandma went to the school and asked my teacher if I failed the class. To her surprise, she learned that I'd done very well, so she could not understand why I cried so much or why I refused to talk to her or my grandpa about it. In fact, my grandpa was the last person I would talk to about anything at that time.

After a couple of days, I warmed up a little. I thought keeping silent would not solve my problem. I had to focus on my plan to run away. I went and told my friend that I was going to run away the next day because I was not sure when my grandpa would execute his plan of forcing me to marry the neighbor's son. My friend cried with me and asked how I was going to go about it. I told her that I planned to run away in the night through the pathway to my father's village, which was about a four or five hour walk from my grandpa's. From there, I would come up with another plan to run away to another place.

She reminded me of how dangerous the pathway was at nights. She came up with a very good plan. She told me to let my grandma and grandpa know that I was going to visit with my parents and my siblings for a couple of weeks and then would return.

When I got home, I told my grandma, and to my greatest surprise, my grandma was fine with my plan. She asked, "Is that why you have been crying so much? You miss your parents and siblings?" I asked her to tell Grandpa, and it was okay with him too.

Leaving Grandpa and Grandma unceremoniously was one of the hardest things I had to do. The decision Grandpa made about choosing a man for me gave me no choice but to keep the secret of leaving them permanently to myself. The journey to my parents' village usually was about a four day wait to get transportation; so I waited. Before then, I got my belongings ready and took them outside as early as possible to wait for the truck on the day. I left some of my things behind because I did not want to give my grandpa and grandma the impression that I was not returning. I packed just the same way I used to when going on holiday to visit with my parents. Only my friend knew my plan was not to return, and she kept it that way. Grandpa gave me my transportation money the night before, which included some spending money, as he always did when I went on holiday.

On the day I was to leave, my friend spent the whole day with me. When it was time for me to catch the truck, she escorted me outside to wait. While we were waiting, we both cried and promised each other to always keep in touch, no matter what, and not to do anything stupid. She gave me some of the money she had saved to add to mine. "You need this more than I do", she said. "I am planning my runaway too but not right now. I still have time to save more money", she added.

The truck finally arrived; it was almost full with market women by the time it got to our area. When it was time for me to go, some of my schoolmates, Grandma, my friend, and other well-wishers in the village surrounded me and the truck. This was usual in the village; you cannot do anything quietly, even if you wanted to. My grandma stood close to me for a few minutes and was kind of teary-eyed. She did that each time I traveled. I, on the other hand, had never shown any emotions or sadness when going to see my parents, but this time was different. I cried like a baby, knowing that I would miss everyone, especially my grandma and my best friend.

Grandpa sat far away on his rocking chair and watched. I ran to him when the driver announced departure time. Grandpa did not show any emotions, as usual. I think it is a man thing, but he had said in the past that he missed me when I was gone on my vacations. So this time I knew he would miss me for a long time, but he did not know that. He asked me to bend down in front of him, and he wished me farewell with the touch of a braided horse tail on my back. He always hung it on his shoulder; sometimes he used it to drive away flies and mosquitoes, but also used it as a whip on me if I failed to listen.

He could not understand why I cried so much this time when I was always happy to go away, but he did not ask me any questions. When I was getting into the truck, I smiled at my well-wishers between tears to hide my mixed feelings of happiness and disappointment with Grandpa. I thought I would have left for high school, in the nearby town or city if the situation had been different. I looked back when I got into the truck and saw everyone waving goodbye; some with smiles as the driver slowly drove away.

I cried out for the driver to stop for a minute, as if I'd forgotten something. When he did, I jumped out of the truck and ran to my friend and held her so tight. She also held on so tight to me, and both of us cried as if we would never let go. My grandma appeared sad at this time. Grandma walked close to me and encouraged me to go back to the truck or the truck would leave without me.

The truck driver was very impatient and honked for me to get back in the truck. I ran back into the truck as I repeatedly yelled out to my friend, assuring her that I would contact her and would never forget her and how much I would miss her. I waved goodbye to Grandma. I could not believe I was leaving the village and everyone for good. But not knowing what my future held and where I was going to end up was always in my mind, even as I waved. I knew that I was going to my parents temporarily, but that was not my long-term plan. Underneath the tears, I was happy to go away from the village, to escape the forced marriage, but on the other hand, I doubted my success. I prayed all the way for God to help me make my plan a reality. As my teacher once told me, "You do not only pray; you work on your plan to make your prayer work. Heaven helps those who help themselves." He said that with prayer and hard work, I could achieve my goal.

We arrived at my parents' village within a couple of hours. Everyone was very happy to see me. The next day I told my mother about my plan to visit with my auntie in the city for a couple of weeks. I begged her to convince Dad to let me go. My dad was fine with this but how was I going to find my auntie? She had moved and they didn't know her current address. I lied to him, saying that I would be able to locate her through her old address and may be through the tenant who lived there now. Big cities in some countries are very busy, with only a few road signs to show directions. Some people build houses without proper access to them. I didn't know if I could even find her old address or if the new tenant would be of any help.

The first time I was in the city I was not allowed to go far away from home. I only ran errands close to home, like going to the nearby market, and I'd only visited with my auntie once. My father suggested that I wait for the next market day. He said, "Market women will be coming to the village market and I will ask them to take you. If you can't locate your auntie, I'll ask the person to keep you with her and return to the village with you the following market day." We both agreed. The fact that my father agreed to my plan and even suggested ways to get there made me so happy. I never thought that he would agree to let me go to the city. I think the reason was because he had not heard from my auntie for some time and wanted to know how she was doing; my return would answer his question.

"Two days to the market day; lucky for me", I thought. I was out visiting with friends, and on my way home, I saw a big trailer parked in front of our house. It was one of our uncles from the city. He'd come to visit with my parents, as he did occasionally. I ran to him and gave him a big hug. I thought of asking him to take me to Auntie in the city, but I did not know how to tell him. I asked my mom to ask my father to do it, and he agreed to talk to uncle about it. Uncle told Dad he would think about it; he might be going to other villages before going back to city to pick up some company equipment; if he did, it would not be possible to take me.

I started praying in my mind for Uncle to decide to go straight back to the city without stopping in the other villages first. Finally, late in the evening, I saw Uncle walking down to our house. He'd gone to speak with his co-driver about getting the equipment and his co-driver had agreed to collect the things in the other villages. That meant it was possible for him to take me. I was so happy upon hearing the news. I told everyone about it, and we were all happy together. As far as my parents were concerned, I was going to the city for a visit, but in my mind, I was going to the city to stay.

CHAPTER
13

My Journey to the City

On the night before I was to leave with Uncle, I was so happy. I packed my stuff and went to bed early, as my dad said that the journey would start in the early morning; it was a long journey to the city by trailer, possibly two days with a big trailer like Uncle's. At the time, the distance or length of travel did not matter to me; all that mattered was that I was leaving the village for good. Uncle came very early in the morning to pick me up, and I was ready for him. I got little sleep during the night, even though I went to bed early, because I was so excited. It was like my dream came true. I prayed all night that Uncle and Father would not change their minds about me going to the city. I kept thinking, "What if my father decides it's a mistake to let me go to the city?"

Still, I was sure that I was on my way to freedom, and I promised to believe in myself and work hard to make things work. As I started the journey, the following gave me hope:

- I believed in my inner strength
- I prayed to God for help, for God answers prayers
- I know I am not alone on my journey, for God is with me
- I trust in God
- Failure comes from fear; I promised to overcome my fear
- I fought for what I want
- I prayed to rise above the expectations Grandpa had for me

- It's a difficult task, but I will try because there is no harm in trying; to not try is to give in to fear; to not try to escape is to give in to a forced marriage
- I have to help myself first because heaven helps those who help themselves

The journey to the city started very early in the morning. I had just finished my breakfast when Uncle came for me. I sat in the passenger's seat beside uncle; he was driving very slowly because of the size of the trailer and the bad condition of the roads. The roads were narrow and full of potholes and at some points busy. The fact that most drivers did not obey the traffic rules made it difficult. Uncle was used to the road, but I was scared. It seemed the journey was longer than I'd remembered. We'd gone in a car the first time, so the journey was smoother and shorter and less stopping on the way. However, Uncle was a very careful driver; he took his time and had a lot of patience.

We stopped a couple of times for meals before dark. When it became very dark and visibility was poor, Uncle told me he was stopping at the next village for rest and would continue in the early morning. When we arrived at the village, it was about halfway to the city. We took shelter in a local guest house. Uncle went straight to one of the rooms and went to sleep immediately. I think he had been there several times before, because it didn't take him much time to settle. I spent half the night chatting and helping one of the young girls who worked for the owner of the guest house. He also was the owner of one of the local restaurants. The guest house and restaurant were open seven days a week, day and night. People hardly drove that road at night due to safety and bad road conditions; drivers used the night to prepare for the next day. I slept during the day in the truck, so I was not sleepy. The fact that I was not familiar with the place made it difficult for me to settle. I was awake almost all night, until about three o'clock, and fell asleep on a bench; there was no room given to me. When I woke up the next morning, I was very sore because the bench was very hard.

A couple of hours later, the girl I had socialized with woke me up and took me to where we could fetch water to bathe. She said Uncle gave her money for two buckets of water; one for him and one for me. Uncle bought rice and fried plantain for us for breakfast, and afterward, we started our journey to the city. Again, it was a very slow journey and very tiring.

We arrived to the city at about midnight. The streets were lonely and quiet; only a few people and vehicles were on the streets. When we got to Uncle's house, I was shocked by the look of it; his house in the village was far better. The house looked so small from the outside; it looked like an old village mound house plastered with cement. It was falling apart and had a half broken entrance. It was interesting to see how many people lived in the small house. There was no running water in the house; the nearest public running water tap was about half a mile away from the house, and sometimes it did not run during the day. People sometimes woke up in the middle of the night to fetch water for use the next day. One of the chores I had to do for my Uncle's wives while I was there was to fetch water from the tap, which was used for cleaning and for other house chores. I did this with the help of Uncle's first wife's sister, who lived with them.

It was a difficult chore. I had to carry a big bucket of water on my head and walk through the street and between running cars and bikes. I did that at least two or three times a day. I wondered how people could live in such an environment in the name of city life. Uncle only rented one side of the house. The city is an expensive place to live, but it is a place where people believe in opportunities. People go to the city from all over Nigeria and some other parts of Africa in search of better lives. When they cannot achieve their purpose, they remain in the city and live in poor conditions. Some work petty jobs that could only pay for their food but not accommodations, and some can only afford poor accommodations.

I only discovered upon arriving at Uncle's house that he had more than one wife, many children, a grown up brother in-law, and a young sister in-law, all living in the small section of the house. Well, that was city life. In some cases, men with two or three wives lived together in a two-bedroom house or apartment in the city due to high rent. When many people live together in a small space, no one has privacy.

When we got to the city, my Uncle promised to take me to Auntie's house within the next three days, but after three days, he started giving me one excuse or another why he was unable to take me to Auntie; from not feeling well, to not having the time, to being tired from his trip and needing to rest. After a week's stay in Uncle's house, I became worried. The foodstuffs my mother had given me for Auntie and my sister were consumed by my Uncle's wives and other family members without my permission. They said the food was going bad, and they did not want it to go to waste.

The first wife was in control of everything in the house, including controlling the second wife, who was much younger than Uncle and his first wife. She was treated like a child and a servant by Uncle and his first wife; she got no respect from her stepchildren either. She had no say about what went on in the house, and she had no money of her own, no freedom, and no friends. She was forced to marry Uncle because her village parent believed Uncle was capable of taking good care of her, and it also would help them out financially.

When Uncle went to work, the first wife took control of the house. I became like a house girl to her; she sent me on errands, even some difficult ones. She woke me in the morning and asked that I assist in bathing her children and get them ready for school, including getting their breakfast and preparing their lunch boxes. She woke me up almost every night to help fetch water for the next day. I had no choice; I did what was asked of me because I did not want to go back to the village.

Uncle did not keep his promise; he changed his story all the time about why he was not able to take me to Auntie and admitted that he was not sure of Auntie's new address, which was the opposite of what he told my father. Uncle traveled a couple of times to the village to drop off some equipment, as usual, and returned with lots of food each time. Some of the food was sent from my parents for my auntie. My parents were not aware that I was still staying in his house because he told them that we arrived in the city safely and that Auntie was fine, which was what my parents wanted to know. He did not tell them that he did not know Auntie's address. I was becoming impatient, as it appeared Uncle was playing games. I continued to wonder how much longer I would stay in his house. The treatment they gave me was terrible; the portions of food they gave me were small, and the quality was not what I was used to. They did not cook separately for me. That is how they cooked, and the portion was the same that they gave everyone. The others were used to it, but I was not. In the village, food was not in short supply; food was in abundance.

I thought I would wait for few more weeks, and if uncle refused to take me to Auntie, I would run away and try to locate her myself. I lost some weight; may be because of the food or just because I was worried. As for food, I was able to buy food from local sellers and hide to eat whenever I was not satisfied with the home food. I became worried and afraid of what would happen to me if he refused to take me to Auntie. I knew where my auntie's husband used to work from the last time I visited with them, and I had my money. I thought maybe I could just take a taxi and go there or take the bus. I thought if I succeeded in locating him, from there he would take me to the house. But I heard horrible stories about taxi drivers kidnapping people, especially young girls in the city. If you were a young gair and unsure of where you were going, you then became a potential target of kidnapping. So I did not want to risk my life. I was not 100 percent sure that he still worked in that location. Regardless of what I was going through, I remained very obedient and respectful to my Uncle and his family because I did not want him to take me back to the village.

One night, a couple of months into my stay in the city, I laid down crying on the mat I was provided with to sleep on at nights; it was like a picnic mat. I cried secretly in the corner of the living room, which was my space at night. The TV room was our bedroom at night; this included Uncle's children and his sister-in-law, each with his or her mat. I turned my face to the wall because I did not want others to see or hear me cry. As I cried, I reprimanded myself for bringing up such a foolish idea of going with Uncle to the city. When things happen, self-blame is very common. On the other hand, how could I have known that things would not work out the way

I'd thought they would? I thought if I had waited for the village market day and followed market women, traders, or even taxi drivers who knew the city very well, maybe the outcome would have be different. Again, I thought it was too late for what it could have been. What is done is done. I could not change anything.

My hope of reuniting with my Auntie faded quickly, also was my strength to pray. I used to pray every night before going to bed; I also encouraged my Uncle's children to join me in prayer as we were taught in school. I was unable to pray as much after a while; all I could pray every night was, "God, please help me to locate Auntie. I don't know what to do or where to go. Please God, help me, and help me not to go back to the village."

That night, I thought of going to the post office to seek help in locating my Auntie's address. That thought faded away quickly, as I did not know how to get to the nearest post office on my own, and as I said, for a young girl who doesn't know where she is going, to take a taxi in city was not easy and sometimes not safe. My hope for God's help also faded. Sometimes you pray and think God is not listening. Because God does not answer you in your own time does not mean he is not listening to your prayers. With what happened next, I have every reason to believe that God answers prayers at the right time.

About two months later, I was outside in the evening and saw someone coming toward me from a distance. As the person walked closer, I recognized him as one of my mother's cousins. When I was sure it was him, I ran to him, greeted him, and hugged him. He was so happy and surprised to see me. I held on to his hand as if I would never let go of him. He asked what I was doing in the city and most especially what I was doing in the area. I told him it was a long story and would not like to discuss it outside, but I told him a little about it.

After walking with him for about ten minutes, he asked me to go back to Uncle's house and let him know that he would stop by to see him after work the next day, which he did. He introduced himself to Uncle and asked for Uncle's permission to take me to his house for a couple of hours to visit. Uncle was fine with it.

During the visit, I told Cousin the whole story and I told him that I didn't want to go back to the village, but Uncle had kept me so long in his house. Cousin felt so bad and expressed disappointment towards my Uncle. "Don't worry about it," he told me. "I will take you to your auntie on the weekend."

I could not wait to get out of Uncle's bondage. "Please let me stay with you until then!" I begged.

He refused. "It would not be fair to leave your uncle and his family unexpectedly", he said. "You need to go back. I will be at the house first thing Saturday morning to take you to your Auntie. And I promise I will see you every evening on my way back from work." He did and sometimes brought me dinner.

On Friday night, the night before the journey to meet my Auntie, I packed all my belongings and waited for my Cousin. He arrived at nine o'clock on Saturday morning with his Beetle car, which he never drove to work because of traffic and the long distance. When it was time for me to leave my Uncle's house, I kind of felt bad because it seemed I had bonded with his children and the second wife. The second wife was more understanding and more generous but could not help to stop the treatment I got from the first wife. In most cases when men are married to more than one wife, the first wife takes control of the others.

My journey started a few minutes after Cousin arrived, with big hugs from everyone in the house. It was a bittersweet good-bye. I missed them all so much. They had become like family, and the children were so fond of me. Some of them followed me wherever I went for an errand. They related to me like their big sister. It seemed I had lived with them for so long, but I could not wait to see my Auntie again.

It took only an hour to drive to my Auntie's house. My Auntie was not at all expecting me. She was not aware that I was on my way to the city. In those days, communication was very difficult. There were no telephones in most houses and absolutely none in the villages. Messages were sent mostly through market men and women (traders) and through the drivers who went there to drop off passengers and traders. There was a bus station and taxi depot, a big terminal for buses and taxies in those days. People went there to ask drivers from the villages if they had any messages for them.

If you received messages from the village frequently, the drivers got to know you and sometimes would deliver mail or verbal messages from your loved ones. You also could mail a letter through the post office, but that would take weeks to arrive, if at all. In my case, my parents did not send any message to my Auntie about my coming to the city because the journey was not planned. They also were sure I was in safe hands with my Uncle, especially when Uncle let them know that we had arrived safely and that he had already taken me to my Auntie.

When we got to my Auntie's house, everyone in the household welcomed us. They were all happy to see me, and I was very happy to see them too. My Cousin spent the whole day with us and left in the late evening. I was very grateful to him.

I explained in detail to my Auntie and her husband how long I had been in the city with my Uncle and his family; they were both surprised and disappointed with my Uncle. My Auntie was expecting a baby at the time. She looked more relaxed and appeared more adjusted than the last time I had seen her; though she said that her struggle with her co-wife had not gone away. She'd been in her forced marriage for a few years, and there were constant fights between her and her co-wife.

When I asked her how she was handling things, she said, "I am here. I have no choice." She said she'd be a lot happier with me there. She told me how much she'd missed me when I went back to the village. The pregnancy suddenly gave her motivation to look forward to a brighter future; It gave her strength and also increased her self-esteem. At least it gave her some sense of belonging and having someone to love.

Auntie had her baby few months after I arrived, and she became a different person; she was very happy. For the first time since she left the village, I saw true happiness in her. Her heart was filled with love. The unconditional love the baby brought to her life was so obvious. Even though she was happy, that did not stop the co-wife rivalry and jealousy.

Co-Wives' Rivalry and Jealousy

J ealousy has been from biblical times or even before. It is more severe in co-wife situations and sometimes leads to hatred. No matter how friendly two women are, once they become co-wives, the friendship stops, and jealousy takes over. As written in Genesis 29:15–35, Laban gave his two daughters, Rachel and Leah to Jacob in marriage, in appreciation for his hard work over several years. The moment the two sisters got married to Jacob, their sisterly relationship was damaged and jealousy became part of their daily lives.

Jealousy triggers negative thinking and insecurity, fear and anxiety for losing something very important to us. If not controlled, it can lead to anger. Jealousy is in all of us; we experience this feeling once in a while and over different things. We show it in different ways. At some point in our lives, we feel a desire to hold on to the things we value so much; a thing or person, and want to have it all to ourselves. If it's impossible to hold on to it, and someone else has it, we become jealous. If it is someone we love, and he or she devotes his or her time to someone else, the jealousy is more intense. This is considered normal, but if we are unable to control our jealousy; it can turn to anger and maybe hatred.

The relationship between co-wives is never associated with true love; it is always with bitter jealousy and sometimes hatred.

There were always fights and arguments between Auntie and her co-wife (jealousy between the two). The joy of a baby did not stop the wives' rivalry. The fights were intense sometimes. Both wives had to be sent away from home to different places to calm down. When this happened, they were each responsible for their own accommodations until they are allowed back home. In most cases, they took shelter in their relatives' homes until such a time when the elders would settle their family problems. These moments were sad and affected everyone in the house.

Whenever they were sent away, their children were not allowed to go with them. The husband kept his children and cared for them, with the help of relatives and house helpers. I usually went with Auntie, even though her husband never asked me to go with her. I had the choice to stay or go, and I felt inadequate when my Auntie was not there.

There were many of those sad times. My Cousin was always our rescue in times of trouble. My Cousin would provide accommodations and food for us in his house until we went back. He was like a father to us and a counselor.

The Effect of Attending Church and Praying

My Auntie did not have many friends. She was not allowed to leave the house, but she was allowed to go to church. I can't remember who introduced her to church, but that contributed to her peace of mind. She attended one of the Aladura churches in the area, which raised her self-esteem. I was very happy that she chose Jesus as her Savior. My Auntie was just like me; we were not brought up as Christians. Our parents never went to church; neither did our grandparents. I only got to know about church and the Bible when I started primary school in the village.

Every school in the village had a church. The school introduced Christianity; it was a mandatory part of the school program. Children were expected to attend church on Sundays. It didn't matter whether or not they believed in it. Bible study was also mandatory.

Every parent who sent their children to school had to agree to allow their children to go to church and Bible study. Looking back, I am happy they did, because it opened many students' eyes and minds to practice Christianity. My grandpa and grandma did not oppose my going to church. Some parents were against this, and some withdrew their male children from school, as they believed that Christianity had come to take their culture away and change the way they did things. It didn't matter so much if their daughters followed Christianity, but they did not want their sons to be part of it. Some fathers regarded their daughters as the property of other men when they grew up and married, so they didn't care whether or not their daughters participated in anything religious. They didn't want their names to be associated with Christianity, and their sons always would bear their names; their daughters would change their last names when they married.

Before I started school, the only thing I knew about Christianity were the celebrations of Christmas and Easter, which everyone celebrated in the village, even if you were pagan or a nonbeliever, except for Jehovah's Witnesses, who did not participate in Christmas celebrations. Christmas was always a big celebration in the village and still is. I always enjoyed the unity that the Christmas holiday brought to families and friends. To me, it was not only about the abundant food; it was the opportunity to visit with other family members and friends and to buy and wear new clothes and shoes. In the village, especially for the less privileged, shopping for clothes and shoes and other materials was done only once a year.

When I finished primary school, I had no reason to continue going to church. It was no longer required of me, and there was no encouragement from my grandpa and grandma. If you dressed for church on Sunday, other than because the school required it, you would get negative reactions and comments from people. Some would asked, if you have nothing better to do with your time. Society discouraged you from practicing Christianity, even if you wanted to. Although there were a few elderly people in the village who practiced Christianity, most of the time they kept to themselves.

Some of the things I learned from attending church and from teachers was to pray for what I wanted while working toward achieving it, and God would grant my request. I was always late to school in those days for no good reason. My grandma always woke me up early, but I found myself falling back to sleep. The teachers warned me on several occasions, but I did not stop. Before we entered the classrooms in the morning, we had to form a line outside in front of the building. This was called assembly, and we then would sing and say the Lord's Prayer; that was also part of the school program, and every student was expected to participate. If any student failed to show up on time for assembly, the student would face consequences. Consequences consisted of being whipped or performing school chores, like cutting grass in the school field, sweeping the school compound, or fetching water from the river for the schoolteachers after school.

I was late to school, as usual, one morning and the teacher ran out of patience with me. They said I had to fetch water from the river for the principal after school. The river was about half a mile from the school. When I reached the principal's house, he noticed that I was crying. I was crying because the bucket of water I carried on my head was too heavy for me, and I was hungry and tired. The principal asked me what was wrong, and I burst out crying and told him. I reminded him that he had asked us to pray for what we wanted and that our prayers would be granted by God. "I've been praying to God to stop me from being late to school, but God did not answer my prayer", I told him. "No matter how early my grandmother wakes me, I'm still late", I added. The funny thing was that our house was opposite the school; the students who lived far away got to school before me.

The principal said, "Listen to me, child. It is one thing to pray and another thing to work hard to achieve your goal through prayer. You don't just pray and expect God to come and do things for you. You have to work hard at what you want in order to make it work"

I took his advice seriously. From that day on, when my grandma woke me for school, I got up immediately and went to the backyard to wash my face with cold water or take a shower right away so that I was able to stay awake. My attendance at assembly was perfect.

The principal called me about three weeks later and commended me for going to assembly and school early. I smiled and told him, "Sir, I am working hard to achieve my goals, and this is one of them. God is helping me. Thank you for your advice."

He said to me, "Keep up the good work, and God will continue to bless you." I worked hard at my goal because I never wanted to fetch water again as a consequence.

I was still not religious for a while after moving to the city. Although I started going to church immediately after I got to the city, I would just sit and listen to the pastor but not retain any information. I was not reading the Bible after church. It is one thing to go to church and another thing to be religious. After some time, I developed interest in the church and participated in lots of activities. I also made friends.

Co-wife jealousy doesn't end because they go to church, but it may give them the wisdom to minimize it. Co-wives' fights, arguments, and jealousy toward each other are very common and are considered the norm and accepted by society.

Most husbands play a part in increasing co-wives' fights, jealousy, and constant arguments. Most husbands are partial and unfair. When there is a fight between wives, the husband takes one's side and abandons the other. He buys more gifts for one than the other and spends more time with one than the other. Women cannot force their husbands to be fair; it has to come from the man. When a husband constantly favors one wife, the other may think he does not love her or that he is charmed (under a spell) by the other wife. Both wives may have reasons to be jealous of each other. The first wife may feel she is losing her husband to another woman and may feel betrayed by her husband. The second wife may feel unwanted and insecure. They end up fighting each other to get what they believe is their entitlement.

Jealousy is more about the fear of the unknown and changes, fear of losing power or control in relationship, fear of insecurity, and fear of abandonment. The first wife may feel her relationship is threatened. No matter the circumstances that lead to women sharing a husband, the co-wife rivalry remains the same. In most cases when there is a fight between the wives, the first wife is the one to report for settlement.

She goes to the elders for fair judgment and to be heard. She asks for her rights. Sometimes the elders are unable to settle the problem and are unable to change the husband's mind. After complaining to the elders without solution, she may try to counsel herself and do things that may bring peace to the house by ignoring her husband's actions and excusing the co-wife's ignorance. This is an effort of a good first wife. She may sometimes manage to get along with the other wife for a while and may lose control some other times.

Women who are in a polygamous marriage say it is very difficult, and it cannot be compared to other marriages. The first wife may feel she is losing control to the other woman and fight to keep her power. The second wife may feel she does not belong and fight to gain some control. Very often, the first wife's focus is only on one aspect of the second wife. She sees her only as a woman who is sharing her husband's love. In some cases, after months and years of fighting each other, they may both realize that they are in the same situation and have nowhere to go. At this point, they may learn to live with one another and tolerate each other. Sometimes the jealousy between co-wives goes deeper and may take them to another level of intolerance.

When one of them strongly believes that her husband does not love her or feels that the husband loves the other woman more than her, she may feel that the other woman is using witchcraft to control her husband.

There are stories of women using witchcraft to bewitch each other due to extreme jealousy in most parts of Africa. It is possible for one of them to take her grievances to a native doctor (juju man or woman). Juju men or women are those with some kind of spiritual or magical power that predicts the future for people and promises them solutions for their problems; just like palm readers. Depending on your belief, their predictions may be true or false. I believe the only one who can predict someone's future correctly is the Almighty God. People who believe in magical powers are mostly led astray. It is not uncommon for a juju man to predict the worst for someone who is already vulnerable and is seeking help. He plays on their weakness. If the juju man knows that a woman seeking help from him has a co-wife, he may tell her that she is cursed or bewitched by her co-wife. He demands lots of money to separate her husband from her co-wife so that she can gain control of her husband and have him to herself.

Once co-wives start listening to a juju person's predictions, they become very suspicious of each other and have a strong belief that their co-wife is bewitching them. This may lead to more hatred and to accusations of witchcraft. The one seeking help from the juju man may believe that the other woman is doing just the same, even though none of the wives is proven to be witch or to have magical power. Each believes in what the juju person is telling them, and they build a wall around themselves that makes them not trust each other.

The problem with co-wives' suspicion or bewitching each other does not end with just the wives; it can be transferred to their children. In some African communities, children's rivalry, hatred, and jealousy can be traced back to co-wives' rivalry, polygamy, and suspicion. For example, a co-wife who believes that her co-wife is bewitching her passes this on to her children and brainwashes them to believe the same. The other woman tells her children the same, and both warn their children not to trust the co-wife. These children transfer the hatred to their siblings. The house may lack unity, and the children may become enemies. By believing their mothers, the children may become very suspicious of their stepmother and her children. This belief is never ending as long as men continue to marry more than one wife. You rarely see a woman in a monogamous marriage accused of witchcraft.

It seems a large number of witchcraft accusations are as a result of co-wives' jealousy in some Africa countries. The extent to which some co-wives hurt each other through witchcraft practices depends on the hatred they have toward each other. Co- wives are blamed for practicing witchcraft or hating each other so much that many fail to look at the fact that the men with multiple wives are creating this problem. They are the root of the so called "evil".

A man who marries more than one wife and puts them together in the same house does not always have peace in his house. If a man must marry more than one wife at a time, it would be wise for him to separate them and spend equal time with them. Some men believe that placing the wives in separate houses can reduce the rate of jealousy, constant fights, and arguments among his wives. They believe the farther away from each other they are, the better it is for all involved. This does not make jealousy go away altogether, but the closer they live to each other, the more problems they encounter and the more witchcraft accusations there are.

Men who put their wives in the same house believe it is better for their children. They believe this promotes unity and love between all members of the family. Putting the wives together may allow them to know each other better, but it does not eliminate co-wife jealousy and hatred. It may help the children relate to each other better, but it does not stop the fights or keeping secrets from each other. The children's unity sometimes depends on how much unity their parents and co-wives have.

Some men put their wives in rooms opposite one another. Although my father married a second wife in his older age, his children were all grown up by then, and his second wife lived many miles away from our house and hardly ever visited my father in our house. We never saw my mother fighting or arguing with her co-wife because they hardly saw each other. That is not to say that the two wives were happy; they were not. Our father's marriage to another wife affected both our mother and all of us.

From the time our father married to the other woman, he became distant to our mother and to us. He was very different from the father we had grown up with. His second marriage may have made him happy in the beginning, but it sure made him unhappy toward the end. Caring for his young children at his old age was not an easy task, physically, morally, and financially. When your father marries another wife, you lose half of him in every way.

My father married a second wife because he wanted more male children; my mother had more female children than male. The second wife had a couple of male children in her previous marriage. My father may have thought she was a male producer and thought she would bear him male children as well. Unfortunately for my father, the woman later gave him three daughters. This shows that we cannot choose for God and should be content with what God gives us. If you think you can afford many wives financially, think of the emotional, physical, and psychological stress this will bring upon you, your wives, and your children.

CHAPTER 15

What Is Witchcraft?

Witchcraft is the practice of magic, especially black magic. Witchcraft is a kind of secret club, with members all over the world; it is practiced by many religions. Witchcraft is the method people use to appeal to what they believe to be a higher power, other than the power of God, to destroy their family or some other members of the community or their properties. It is called different names and is practiced differently from culture to culture and from country to country. For example, in Brazil, it is Mocumba; in Jamaica, it is Obeah; in Haiti, it is Voodoo; in some parts of Nigeria, it is Juju.

Many who believe in witchcraft believe it works to their benefit and provides them with the protection they need and the power to control others. Some societies believe that witches possess power to do good and evil, but many practitioners use it to do more evil than good. However, there is a big stigma that goes with the name witch or wizard. Once anyone is believed or suspected to be a witch or wizard, he or she is hated by the community. Every bad thing that happens in their families or in society is blamed on them, even if they know nothing about it.

Before the modern medicine, many people worldwide believed in witch doctors to cure them of their illness. In some parts of Africa, some witches performed miracles and rituals and still do, healing people and not using it only to destroy. In most part of the world in the past, people got help from the witches for their benefits. Those that practiced it for good were called cunning men, white witches, or wise men. Some witch doctors used their power and rituals to help people in their communities and saved many lives before the use of English medicine.

Good witch doctors or voodoo men and women cured the sick with herbs and eased the pain of dying people by their powers. Remember that they can use their power for both good and bad. They also practiced and performed the work that doctors and midwives now do, though in their own primitive ways. Not all witches use their power for selfish reasons or to hurt people. While some use their energy to do harmful things, others helped people. Those involved in bad practices sought power from Satan and worshipped the devil. Witchcraft practice has had both pro and con effects in religious and traditional medicine in all cultures. In the rural areas in some parts of Africa, people still seek help from juju people to cure the sick, especially where there is no hospital or where English medicine is not within their reach. If witchcraft is used for good things, it is call science or technology, and if it is used for bad things, it is called black magic or voodoo.

Do Witches Exist and Are They Real?

People's belief in witches and witchcraft is very strong in many communities in Africa, even though there is no scientific proof. Even intelligent people still believe in the existence of witchcraft. Many people believe that witches do exist and are real, and some others believe it is not real; others call it magic.

People's belief in witchcraft in this society is as strong as the belief people in most countries or communities have about the soul leaving the body and surviving outside of the body. Even though there is no scientific proof about this, people's belief is very strong, and changing these people's minds to believe otherwise is almost impossible. Your belief, your culture, your upbringing, and your experience in life will best answer your question. To deny the existence of witches and wizards is to deny the existence of demons and the devil, and to deny the power of witches and wizards is also to deny the power of Satan.

The majority of these witches choose the evil part because of the quick financial gain associated with it, instead of doing the right thing. It is easier for many to follow the wide road that will lead them to hell than to be patient and wait for God's time. Most times, the decision people make leads them to destruction, desertion, and poverty later on. When someone invites evil power, what they get may be destructive power they cannot control.

Some groups of people are accused of witchcraft more than others, and it is more commonly practiced in some societies than others. Witchcraft is practiced by men and women, but mostly the elderly women are accused of witchcraft. Sometimes children are also accused. From the time of Adam and Eve, women were believed to be Satan's agents and with evil minds, and they are regarded as less than men in all aspects of life. Among people believed to be witches and wizards, women rate the highest number, and these numbers are higher in Africa. Women are also known as the best practitioners, even from centuries ago. Women are also believed to be the leaders of the practitioners. No one knows why people practice witchcraft. Some believe it may be due to some form of sickness, idle minds in some women, idle minds and dementia in elderly, or the devil's work and some kind of disability among children in some societies. Some believe that extreme jealousy in women (especially women of polygamous marriages), inequality in women, depression, and anger, may be some of the reasons women take part in practicing witchcraft. Children born with certain disabilities may be a target due to their behavior, which is different from other children. They are called names and are isolated, and sometimes they are beaten for things they know nothing about. Children born with some form of disability are treated badly in some cultures, or even worse, they are not given a chance to participate in any activities in their communities; most times they stand alone.

In most African countries, when a child is born different from others (with some type of disability), especially when the mother dies giving birth, society condemns the child. The community or members of the family believe that the child is a witch or wizard and has brought bad luck to the family and may have caused his or her mother's death. They may kill the child or refuse to feed him or her, thus starving him or her to death. If the child grows up and behaves differently from other children due to his or her disability, they may beat and threaten the child to confess to witchcraft. After the confession, the family may decide whether to stone the child to death or take the child to the voodoo doctor, who they believe can cure the child of the evil spirits. In some cases, if members of the family believe that witchcraft is passed onto a child by her mother or a close member of the family as revenge, both the mother and the child will receive the same punishment, which is harsh.

Children, the elderly, and women from poor homes are most often accused. The way they look and act is enough reason to target them, even if they are intelligent. They are only accused by their looks and behavior, which may be the same as other children, even if their look is as a result of sickness.

For example, I knew of a family whose child was behaving strangely, different from other children in the family. This child would wake up in the middle of the night and walk around, eat, and sometimes destroy things when others were asleep. When asked the following day what happened, she would deny getting up. Her condition deteriorated to the point of her opening the door and walking outside at night, though she would come back before everyone woke up, and she would fall asleep immediately. The family would discipline her, sometimes severely. As she grew older, her condition got worse. The parents sent her to their village and labeled her as a witch. A few months later, the news arrived that she was dead.

I learned about sleepwalking when I came to Canada, and thinking back, the little girl may have suffered from a sleepwalking disorder or a type of mental illness that caused her to behave differently from other children. Instead of her parents seeking help for her, they sent her away, where she later died

In most cases, society condemns such children instead of seeking help for then. If the child is from a polygamous marriage, this further gives the mother's co-wife a weapon to accuse her of witchcraft. The helpless mother may not have money to treat the child in the hospital; she may seek the easy way out; help from the juju doctor. In some countries, women of polygamy are more frequently accused of seeking help from voodoo doctors because they believe the voodoo doctor will help solve their problems, and the cost is cheaper than hospital costs.

Consulting voodoo practitioners is not only common to polygamy. Many people in the rural areas and some people in the city still rely on the juju doctors to help them out when they are in trouble and when they are sick. Some are said to get good results, and others are not so lucky. It is like going to a medical practitioner to get a prescription for medication. In some cases, the medication that worked for one person may not work for another, even with the same type of sickness. Christians are also known to pay visits to juju men and women.

CHAPTER 16

Rituals (Christianity and Witchcraft)

Many believe that witchcraft is only practiced by pagan religions, but witchcraft and invocation of evil spirit is not peculiar to paganism. It also exists in all religions and denominations. In many countries, some Christians and people of other religions are known to be Satan's agents. Some pastors and church leaders hide under the Bible to manipulate their members to commit crimes; they use their evil power to take advantage of the vulnerable people and cover up with the Bible. They also brainwash and deceive their followers and take advantage of the poor and the needy. In order for some to get power, they make a deal with the devil. In most cases, what they get in return is more trouble. It is alleged that some denominations of Christians are ritualistic; just like witches and wizards, and some use their demonic powers to destroy others.

People who seek help from the devil to solve their problems invite trouble and do not have peace in their lives. There is no love or peace in a house controlled by the devil. As written in the Bible, there is no peace with people who invoke and seek the evil power. "'Are you coming in Peace?' Jeram asked Jehu. 'How can there be peace?' Jehu answered, 'When we still have all the witchcraft and idolatry that your mother Jezebel started?'" (2 Kings 9:22). Saul died because he was unfaithful to the Lord. He tried to find guidance by consulting the spirits of the dead instead of consulting the Lord (1 Chronicles 10:13). God also punished Saul.

Some denominations of Christians cast spells with the power they get from the devil instead of consulting with God; just like witches and wizards do. The problem with getting power from the devil is that the devil does not give freely. The devil takes more from his agents than he gives. God gives without expecting anything in return. Some denominations of Christians worship just the same way witches and wizards do. Some denominations also use candles, the Bible, incense, and chants. Witches uses candles, wood, chants, bones, incense, and rhymes as well. Witchcraft can be practiced just as Christianity is practiced.

Rituals and spells have been in practice even before biblical times. This is also mentioned in the Bible in Leviticus 14:2–25. Cedar wood, birds, hyssop, and water were also used for ritual purification, which some denominations of Christians uphold till this day.

Lots of churches are governed by corrupt pastors who take power from juju men or women and preach what they want people to hear. They worship money, hide behind Satan, and put on a clean gown and hold a Bible to deceive their congregations. They close their eyes to the truth; they see wrong things that the rich people are doing and praise them because they want the rich men's money. They discriminate against the poor, even by their preaching. They worship those who can donate big money, and they pay little or no attention to the poor or low-income earners.

Rich Pastors, Poor Congregations.

The action of some pastors is not any different from that of corrupt rulers or leaders. Some corrupt rulers claimed to love their country and their people but do nothing for them.

They take their families out of the country they claimed to love so much to a civilized country for better lives, and they embezzle the money meant to help their communities and send the money for the maintenance of their family abroad. They neglect children and the poor and put themselves in power, over and over, using the money meant for their people and their communities. They buy mansions abroad and leave their people in shacks. They make empty promises all the time and kill those who challenge their authority; they get away with murder. They enjoy the light abroad and leave their people in darkness in their own countries. Many pastors pray to cast out hatred, demons, and darkness in other people, even when they have hatred in them.

Remember that there is a judgment day for everyone; a day when we shall be accountable for our actions. Some pastors make themselves kings over others. Some of their power comes from Satan. They praise themselves, condemn others, and issue a certificate of glory to themselves. They make themselves the judge of men. They feel strongly that they are going to heaven and others are going to hell. Remember that your sweet tongue, deception, manipulation, and using the Bible and God's name to cover up your evil deeds will not take you to Heaven; just like people using witchcraft to destroy people; they will not make it to Heaven. You cannot make it to Heaven just because you are a pastor. The only thing that may take you there is your good work on earth.

The following are some of the things that I feel may take you to Heaven:

- You admit you are a sinner
- You are not working in your name but in Christ's name
- You serve no other God but the Almighty God
- You do not serve God and Satan at the same time
- You believe Jesus is the Son of God and your Savior
- You have accepted Jesus's sacrifice for your sin
- You have put your trust in Jesus and follow his instructions
- You do unto others as you would like them to do unto you
- You are not jealous of people who are progressing more than you
- You are not praying to put others down
- You treat the rich and the poor the same
- You leave an exemplary life
- You do not become a pastor with the intention of getting money from people
- You don't hide under God's name and serve idols
- You love unconditionally
- You preach peace and not hatred

- You do not use evil magic to perform miracles
- You worship God and not money
- You do not make yourself the king over others
- You do not preach peace and practice hatred at the same time

Do you think you can make it to heaven with evil ways? If you think so, good luck. If you don't think so, it is not too late to change your ways. God forgives sinners. We are all sinners.

Some pastors try to live what they believe is a spiritual life that is not God's command. They worship Satan secretly and praise God outwardly. Their tongues are like the tongue of Satan. They deceive people with their sweet words. They use the choices God gave them to choose evil. God gave us choices, hoping we will make right choices. For many, they make wrong choices. Remember that God gave Adam and Eve the same choices. When Adam was tempted by Satan in the garden, Adam made the decision to listen to Satan and did exactly what Satan asked him to do. God told Adam and Eve, "If you eat from the tree of the knowledge of good and evil, you will surely die," but Satan told them the opposite of what God said; "You will not surely die. The day you eat from the tree of good and evil, you will become like God."

Unfortunately, Adam and Eve believed the sweet and deceitful words of Satan, rather than the words of God, and they ate the fruits of knowledge; good and evil. The consequence was as God told them, and from that day on, they shall die. Jesus was tempted by the same Satan but chose to obey the words of God and ignored Satan.

Be a true man of God; live by what you preach. Do not live a life of a man with multiple wives with divided love. Do not use control and magic power over your members just because you are the head. As stated in Ephesians 5:23, "But headship is no license for tyranny."

Some pastors feel they can control their congregations, just as some African men feel it is their right to control their wives. In most African countries, culture and tradition influence control and behavior in men. They feel men are superior to women and should have control of their lives. Women are powerless and remain under the control of their husbands. When there are co-wives, both their powers are also taken away; even the right to speak. Instead of a jealous co-wife to turn her anger on her husband for marrying a second wife or, in some cases, for breaking the promises he made to her when they were married, she turns her anger to her co-wife. She is afraid to talk to her husband about issues that bother her or just to tell him that what he did was wrong. Her controlling husband may threaten to divorce her if she should say anything.

In times of trouble with his wives, the man with plural wives runs away from home and from his problems, instead of facing the situation head on. Running away does not solve any problem; it sometimes compounds it. Some men feel because they are the head of the house, they can use this as a license to control their wives. These husbands should remember that he is "one flesh" with his wife and should "honor her and consult her on family matters." Men already in plural marriages should also love their wives in order to get the satisfaction of a good marriage that mostly exists in monogamy.

In polygamous marriages, co-wives' conflict is the biggest problem women face; it is like fighting a war without ending and is often associated with physical fights, arguments, and violence. Extreme co-wife jealousy will only end when men stop marrying more than one wife.

CHAPTER 17

Men and Control

Controlling husbands, in some cases, are weak, insecure, and ungrateful and do not know how to deal with marital issues. The only way they know is by control. Many marriages fail due to the husband's inability to take charge of his household. This sometimes is due to weakness or an inability to run a home.

A reasonable husband needs to take charge of his home, especially his children, and he is to be fair to his wife. He is not to leave his responsibilities to his wife/wives but share in the upbringing, discipline, and direction of his children. He is to be there for his children no matter what. Some men use work as an excuse not to support their family, physically or otherwise. They complain of being tired after a day's work and feel they should not take part in anything that goes on in the house. I think this is wrong. A woman performs her duties, even after her day's work, trade, or even factory job, without complaining. Husbands should do the same. This is not to say that women should compete with their husbands, but a husband's support can be appreciated, and it brings happiness to the family.

Some men spend little time with their children. These fathers may say they earn the income in the family and can only provide financial support; the rest is left for their wives. Some say they work far from home, which gives them little time to spend at home with their family. If their time at home is spent wisely, they can still have a few quality hours each day with their children. Some of these fathers work closer home but prefer to spend time socializing and drinking with their friends after work, just to avoid coming home early to be with their families. You can be home for only a few hours and still make a positive impact on your family.

Most children raised in polygamous homes do not know their fathers very well. This is also observed in monogamous homes, but it is more common in polygamous homes. Some of these children have a minimal relationship with their father, as their fathers don't spend enough time with them to teach them what they should know. Sometimes their children have to learn responsibility from other people, as their fathers failed to teach them.

Lack of quality time spent with their children has a negative impact on some children throughout their lives. Neglecting your children is a form of emotional abuse. Any child or children who grow up in an abusive home, for example, may become abusive themselves, thinking it is the right thing to do. Some of these children may lack communication and social skills with their children and wives when they grow up because they were not taught these skills.

Some fathers do not show affection and love to their wives and children, or they may find it difficult to engage in useful communication with their children. Children who grew up with little or no affection shown to them find it very hard to be affectionate with their own children. The few hours these fathers stay home with their children is spent picking on the bad things their children do and what the wives didn't do well and punish them for everything. The fathers hardly ever praise them for the good things they do. Some pay little attention to what goes on in the house.

Keeping distance from children is accepted in some cultures and is taken as the role of a good father. Some controlling fathers find it hard to socialize with their children, especially their female children, as this is also taken as a norm. In some other cases, the culture promotes harsh punishment and fathers' authority over their children and wives, to the extent that some caring fathers are afraid to support their wives physically in caring for their children because of what their extended family members will say or think about them. Sometimes when a caring father is seen playing or caring for his children and helping his wife/wives, people frown upon him and call him names like "baby sitter" or "woman wrapper." His friends may avoid him because he is helping his wife and children and no longer has time to socialize with them.

It is your responsibility as a father to communicate effectively and take care of your children and wife/wives. If you are not sure what to do, you can learn from a responsible father how to parent. Then show and teach it to your children, especially your sons, as lots of African men have no father figures or role models growing up. Start teaching your children responsibilities when they are very young. Sons do copy what their fathers do.

The time spent teaching your children can also be a fun time and an opportunity to know your children better. It will also improve your communication with them. Sometimes it doesn't take much. A technique that works is praising your child when he is finished with the assigned chores, even when the chores he does are not as perfect as you would want them to be. Even if you are busy, create time for your children, and be appreciative of their efforts. In some cultures, fathers find it easier to condemn than to praise. Be your children's hero and not a disappointment. Never neglect your children.

CHAPTER 18

Be a Responsible Father and Husband

A responsible father does not neglect his family and please outsiders, just to promote himself. Treat your family fairly and respectfully. It is better to gain the love of your family and be happy with yourself than to win a village and be unhappy. True love is that which you get from your family. Friends come and go, but family, in most cases, remains the same.

"It is better to eat a dry crust of bread with peace of mind than to have a banquet in a home full of trouble" (Proverbs 17:1). When fathers neglect to fulfill their responsibilities to their children, they have neglected sacred responsibilities that can have eternal consequences. Do your best, and pray that God will help you.

Life is full of ups and down, even within the family. No one is hanging without climbing a ladder or a rope to get there. You must be proud of your children and want them to succeed in life. But you must sacrifice your time for them when they are young.

I had been in the city for a couple of years, as my Auntie and her husband allowed me to stay with them. One day, I went to the market to buy few things for my Auntie. On my way back from the market, one of my Auntie's maids ran toward me with excitement and said, "Your father is here from the village for a visit! I am so happy to see him!"

I was so shocked that I froze for a moment. I was not sure whether to drop the stuff I was carrying and run or brave it and welcome my father. I did not want the maid to know that I had been avoiding my father, so I thanked her for coming to me with the news. I let her know that I would be with my father as soon as possible, after I took what I had bought to the kitchen. I must have spent more than thirty minutes in the kitchen, just thinking of how I was going to face my father. I wondered what his intentions were.

I finally put myself together. I thought, This is the city. My father does not have power or control over things. I welcomed my father, who was very happy to see me; in fact, I was happy to see him too. My father, Auntie, and I spent some time talking about family and my siblings at home. I also asked about my grandparents, which he stated were doing very well. That evening, after my Auntie's husband returned from work, I saw my father, Auntie, and her husband having a meeting. I didn't know for certain, but I had the feeling it was about me. I became restless and wanted to know what was discussed at the meeting.

Later, my Auntie told me that Father wanted me to go back to the village in a couple of days.

"What did you tell him?" I asked in a hurry.

My Auntie smiled and said, "Don't worry. Over my dead body will your father take you to the village, and over my dead body will I let your father or any other person treat you the way my father treated me. And my husband is on my side."

I was very happy to hear this.

The following day, I went to see one of our Uncles who lived far away from my Auntie. Everyone went to him for help and with complaints because he was a tough man and well respected by the family members, even by my father. He had a positive effect on people. Even though my Auntie supported my staying with her in the city permanently, I felt it would register in my father's head if someone as powerful as my Uncle talked to him. My Uncle had the wisdom and maturity to deal with sensitive issues. I was glad that he sided with me too. He asked me to invite my Father to his house the next day.

"I prefer that your father come to my house," he said, "as this will give us quiet time together to talk."

The next day, my father and I went to my Uncle's house. I never told my father that I'd complained to Uncle. I only told him that Uncle requested his presence and wanted to use the opportunity to visit with his family. My father was happy at the chance to see him after a long time. My Uncle was always busy in the city and hardly visited home, and when he did, he only visited in the city and not in the village.

My Uncle was very aware of Auntie's situation and the negative impact the forced marriage had in her life. He stated he never wished for the same to happen to me or to anyone else in the family. My Uncle had a lengthy discussion with my father. I was not told in detail what was discussed; the only thing that was important to me was that my father was asked to go back to the village without me and to let the man with whom he had the marriage deal know that I was never going to marry him.

When we were leaving my Uncle's house, he tapped me on the shoulder and smiled. He said, "Don't worry dear, you are not going back to the village with him, and you are not going to marry that man. Your father will deal with the mess he created."

I was so happy, and to my surprise, my father took it very well; he was not upset. He left for the village a couple of days later and corrected his wrongs about the arranged marriage, and that was the end of it. That was also the end of my father interfering in my marriage life and that of my siblings.

This brings about the question of what a father's role is in raising his female children, especially a poor father. Does he bring female children into this world as a trade object, just to free himself of financial burdens?

A father's role in raising children is a big responsibility, especially when the children are young. The task of raising and educating children is challenging and costly, but not educating your children is even more costly and damaging to the children. If you are not a good role model to your children, your children's chances of succeeding in life may be limited. You are like the mirror in which they see themselves and are their first teacher. You should teach your children right from wrong when they are young. Raising sons should not be different from raising daughters, especially at a young age.

The different treatment sons and daughters receive from their fathers stands out in most African countries. Many fathers give their sons preferential treatment, and they treat their daughters poorly. Culturally, some fathers do not see anything wrong with treating their daughters different from their sons. Some fathers only parent according to their own upbringing and do not know any better. Some fathers grow up believing that control is the best way to parent.

A good father can be strict but harmless and can also be his child's best friend. Your children should not be afraid of you. They should be able to talk to you freely at any time and about anything, even about sensitive issues. Your children will be grateful and respectful to you at all times if you show them respect. Regardless, there is no excuse for cruelty toward your children, especially daughters.

Like everything in life, failure comes from not knowing what to do, lack of education, not doing what is right, and controlling. This also applies to raising children. Some parents treat their daughters and sons equally and are happy with the positive results later in life. Others regret the way they treated their children. If you are one of those who regret raising your children the way you did (which had a negative impact on your children), it may be because of some of the following reasons:

- You imposed your rigid traditional ways on them
- You disconnected and kept your distance from your children

- You put them down for every little thing, instead of praising them when they did well and when they deserved to be praised
- You refused to educate them
- You waited for miracles to happen in their lives, instead of working hard to improve their lives
- You wished for an easy life for your children instead of contributing to make it happen for them
- You expected them to love you when you did not show them love
- You were dishonest to them, instead being open
- You forced them to marry at an early age to avoid your responsibilities
- You left the responsibilities of raising your children to your wife
- You ignore your children most times instead of listening to them

For some, it is never too late to correct the wrong. If you have to raise your children all over again or you are still raising children, you will have to do the following:

- Change from your traditional rigid ways and not impose your cultural beliefs on them
- Connect with them more instead of distancing yourself from them
- Do more praising instead of putting them down and condemning them for every little mistake
- Educate them instead of forcing them to marry a stranger of your choice for your financial gain
- Do not wait for an easy life for your children when you didn't contribute to their well-being
- Show them love and how to love
- Be honest with your children and your wife instead of keeping secrets from them
- Be part of their lives instead of avoiding them
- Be a trusted friend to your wife and children

"Teach your child how he should live, and he will remember it all his life" (Proverbs 22:6).

Part of your job as a father is to raise your children with God's instructions and show them love and how to love others. If you are a Christian, bring your children up with Christian beliefs and discipline. If you are not a Christian, bring them up with discipline according to your religion, but never hurt them or deny them education and other important things they need. Again, you need to discipline your children in a proper manner while they are young. Discipline your children while they are young enough to learn (Proverbs 19:18). If you don't, you are helping them to destroy themselves. If your child is brought up well, he/she will care for you in your old age, as it is expected by most African cultures.

If you want your children to take care of you when you are old, invest in them and take care of them while they are young.

The above guideline for fathers does not mean that you must not discipline your children in a proper manner. It does, however, condemn any act of abuse and neglect. Know there is a difference between the two. Teach your children, by good example, how you want them to live. In most cases, you get back what you put out. If you grow a good seed and care for it, it will bring good fruits when the time comes. Cooked seeds never grow or bring fruit. "If you sow the seed of injustice, disaster will spring up, and your oppression of others will end." Raise your children well so you can be proud of them, as God is with Jesus. This includes discipline in a respectful manner.

Discipline is a good way to teach your children good behavior and how to get along with people and respect others, but you should not use harsh punishment. If you use harsh punishment to teach your children, they may rebel and develop bad attitudes. Children would develop better attitudes if fathers would ask their wives to assist in the discipline and parenting of their children and do so in a gentle manner. Below are some things you should have in mind when disciplining your children:

- You have to discipline yourself before you can discipline your children
- Most children are well behaved when disciplined in a gentle manner, rather than punishment
- Show them love, even when disciplining them
- Set reasonable rules for them
- Do not lose your temper, even if they don't meet your expectations
- Be patient, as patience gives good results
- Set rules; if rules are not followed, you can then discipline and correct them in a gentle manner because bad behavior deserves discipline
- Seek help from professionals and other responsible parents who know how to parent, if needed; the best advice may come from a parent who knows what to do
- Do not confuse discipline with punishment; they are not the same.
- Use kind words when talking to your children, and always remind them how much you love them
- Show your love and affection to your children by your words and deeds
- Encourage good behavior by showing them the same
- You must be able to please your family first before others
- Don't try to be a super daddy; sometimes you cannot do it alone; apply your wife's wisdom, for that is why God made her your wife; to support you.
- Be a good father

A good father is the one who knows the value of education and provides same for his children.

He does not use his harmful traditional practices to entrap or deprive his children of his fatherly love.

He develops and brings up his children in the way Jesus developed wisdom.

He puts God first and *never neglects his children.*

He holds up to his responsibilities and provides for his children.

He is ready for the challenges that come with being a father and will face them head on.

He is responsible for his children even in time of trouble, for sickness and good health

He is not abusive to his children but is a spiritual leader at home.

He takes responsibility for his actions and does not lay blame on his children or wife for his wrongdoings.

CHAPTER 19

Honor-Killing in Forced Marriage

Child abuse involves children all over the world, but especially female children in most African countries. Another terrible act of abuse in some African countries is the art of honor-killing. This is not peculiar to Africa; it is also happening in the civilized world. Those that happen in the Western world are as a result of immigrants from the countries where it is practiced. In most parts of the world, there is no explanation for the terrible crime committed against women and children by their fathers. In this, there is not enough awareness about child abuse. In most cases child abuse is not reported or is not taken seriously by authorities. In some other countries, it is an abomination for children to report their parents to the authorities for abuse or other wrongdoings. It is also forbidden for women to report their husbands. Children and women take abuses as the norm in these cultures. The authorities fail to recognize the abuse and don't provide victims with the support needed. Abuse of women and female children is more common in some countries, cultures, and communities than others. Many families who emigrate from other countries to the Western world come with their cultural beliefs. There have been many cases of young girls from these cultures being murdered by their fathers over the years in the name of honor-killing and other forms of domestic violence. Though the law in some countries prohibits these acts, they do little or nothing to prevent it or to protect the lives of the victims.

A good father must be a good husband first, before he can be a good leadership figure in his society.

A good father must not practice the rules of the ancient civilization, where women had no rights, and men had every right. Under the ancient civilization in many countries throughout the world, a woman was referred to and treated as a thing; she was the property of her husband, just as he owned other materials and animals. The moment she got married, she was imprisoned by her husband she was never allowed to leave him or even to leave the house. She is forbidden from seeking divorce; only her husband can divorce her when he wants.

A woman was regarded as a housewife. She was to stay home and cook, clean, take care of her children, and serve her husband, and her duty was to take orders from her husband and to obey his commands. A woman who followed her husband's orders without question or argument was regarded as a good housewife. If a woman disobeyed her husband, she would be put to death in any way the husband wished, and no punishment would come to her husband.

These women were controlled to the point that they could not speak for themselves or even ask for clarification when told to do things. Today, a few women are gaining independence and are able to contribute or make

111

suggestions to their husbands, but a lot more needs to be done to give voices to other millions of women and to gain independence. Before now in some Africa cultures, a husband could kill his wife over little things, and he would not be punished. This is still happening in some countries today.

A woman was only good enough to give birth to her children but was not able to have a say on what happened in the children's lives. She and the children remained at the mercy of her husband. If a woman died during labor, her husband would immediately replace her, much as he replaced his other property. A wife was forbidden from getting married for many years after the death of her husband, if at all.

Honor-killings date back to ancient societies and has been a practice ever since in some countries. It is a societal norm in which men were given all power, and women were denied rights. Social power, political power, and economic power belonged to men. Many parents in the Western world or in countries were it does not apply find it hard to believe that fathers, parents, and close family members would kill their own daughters or sons because the child's behavior was believed to have brought shame to their family. It is even more surprising that parents would sacrifice the lives of their children to save themselves from shame. People who practice this call it a traditional practice and they do not want this to end in their lifetime. Many are also influencing their children with their beliefs.

Some parents believe it is the right thing to do and say they are following the words of the Bible. They also believe it is their right to decide what happens to their children, including taking their children's lives if their children are proven stubborn.

If a man has a son who is stubborn and rebellious, a son who will not obey his parents (even though they punished him), his parents were to take him before the leaders of the town where he lived and make him stand trial. They were to say to them, "Our son is stubborn and rebellious and refuses to obey us; he wasted our money and is a drunkard." Then the men of the city were to talk to him. If he did not listen to them, they were to stone him to death to get rid of this evil. "Everyone in Israel will hear what has happened and be afraid" (Deuteronomy 21:18–21).

They claimed they had every right to do anything they wanted with their children, as the Israelites were given the right over their children in ancient time. The message is that you are not living in the ancient time. Things have changed, even in the New Testament.

Honor-killing is the homicide of a member of a family or social group by other members; because they believe that the victim has brought shame or dishonor to their family or community. Unfortunately, it affects young girls more than boys in almost every country that practices it.

The belief–that honor-killing is often associated with just some religions or cultures is not true; it is happening in a lot of cultures. These practices are stronger in some religions, countries, cultures, and communities than others. A woman found guilty of adultery or suspected of having a relationship with another man in some societies could be enough reason for her husband to kill her and get away free in the name of honor. In some countries, being raped was seen as a disgrace, to the point of killing the girl or woman victim.

The fact that the government does nothing to protect the lives of the victims further puts them at risk. Instead of protecting the victims, they protect the abuser, and the police, in some cases, do the cover-up. If men cheat in these communities, it does not mean anything, but when women cheat, it may mean a life sentence for the women. They can kill her without giving her a chance to defend herself. By doing this, they remove the stain on their family honor. They believe it is better to kill the woman to clean their honor than to face the shame. It is alarming how many countries still practice honor-killings.

When people who practice honor-killings immigrate to other countries, they take their rigid traditional practices with them and think they can practice it anywhere.

In some countries in Africa, there are many ways families kill their children or family members, especially female children who they believe brought dishonor to their family. Many cases of honor-killings are arranged to look like accidents. In this case, the family members do not directly kill the victim themselves, in order to avoid jail time.

In some cases, the family asks their young children to commit honor-killings because the law allows convicted minors to serve time in juvenile jail. They are freed after few months if the offense committed takes place before the age of sixteen. Sometimes if the crime takes place in the village, the criminal is not even convicted. The elders in this case use traditional law to punish the criminal. Sometimes the punishment is as light as receiving twenty four strokes of a cane. Behavior that supports honor-killings are very pronounced, even among the young people, especially boys.

Although honor-killings is an oppression of women, parents believe they are removing the stain brought about by their daughters. After killing their daughter, they remove everything that belonged to her and forbid mention of her name, as mentioning her name is a reminder of the shame she once brought to the family. Other siblings are warned not to behave in a way close to their late sister's and are told if they do, they will be killed just like her. They do everything in their power to make it look as though she never existed.

Many people believe that these types of crimes are committed by non-Christians and pagans; this is not the case. Honor-killings have no tie to religion; this was practiced before any organized religion. It affects men and women. A man can also be a victim of honor-killings by members of the woman's family if he is caught having an inappropriate relationship with a virgin other than his wife or with a married woman. This is rare, but it does happen. In some cases, if children of certain cultures participate in other cultural activities or religion, this can also be enough reason for the family members to kill them. Some immigrants, especially the men, do not leave their practices, including honor-killings behind when coming to another land.

Some of these men bring their wives and daughters to other countries in the same way they brought other materials, and they treat them the same. They would be surprised when the law of their new country persecutes them when they are caught practicing such an unlawful act called honor-killing. In civilized countries, lots of women are beaten or hurt every year because of honor-killings by immigrants, and the crimes are covered up sometimes by family members. Some of the crimes are not brought to court, or if they are, the cases are dismissed due to lack of evidence.

In some communities, family honor is more valued than safety or the lives of their children and women. In some countries in the Middle East, men are allowed to kill their wives for adultery, and when they do, they receive light sentences or no sentence if he can prove he killed her to defend his honor. However, some countries even in the Middle East have made efforts toward giving more severe punishment to men who kill their wives and daughters for honor; even then, a lot more needs to be done to get through to the people in these communities, especially the uneducated men.

Honor-killings have increased in some countries instead of decreasing, even in civilized countries, and it is not slowing down due to poverty. The most unfortunate thing is that women are the biggest target.

Girls and women will forever remain victims of honor-killings in many countries if they do not get help, as they are expected to totally depend on their husbands. In these societies, women are seen as their husband's property, with no identity and no voice of their own. They are not allowed to cry out or report abuse.

Afraid to Report Honor-Killings

Many cases of honor-killings are not reported because the cases are not taken seriously by the law of the countries that practice it and because the authorities fail to prevent these killings by not protecting women. The law is in place in these countries, but it works against women. These societies also support men by not taking crimes committed against women seriously. In some cases, police side with men and always take the killings of women as a domestic violence, and they do nothing about it.

Women in some societies have no freedom. As children, they are controlled by their fathers, and as wives, they are enslaved by their husbands. Worst of all, society sees them as just women. Many girls are choosing drastic measures to avoid forced marriages.

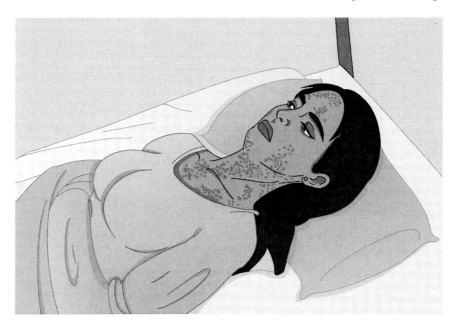

Many girls have committed suicide by setting themselves on fire, overdosing on medication, and hanging themselves. Even with this, many parents are adamant that they are doing the right thing in the name of culture and honor.

Some hospitals in Africa are overwhelmed with the number of girls that are rushed for treatment on a daily bases. This type of story is not in the past; it is still happening. Some parts of African countries are well known for their brutality against wives and daughters. In these countries, murders and other crimes committed by forced marriages and honor-killings are becoming the norm.

There was a story of a beautiful young girl who committed suicide by jumping into a well to escape the brutality from a man she was forced to marry. Her story is one of those that turned deadly. This incident happened years ago in the next village to my grandparents' village where I grew up. Similar things are still happening in villages today.

The circumstances that lead to her death were told to me by one of her younger sisters years later, during one of my visits home. I knew the girl who committed suicide, as she stayed with her grandparents in the same village as I did. Her sister visited with her a few times while I was in the village. Her sister and I were happy to see each other again after a long time. After hugging and joking about the past, I asked her about her sister. She became quiet and paused for a moment. She then asked me quietly to give her my address so she could pay me a visit. She wanted to talk in private, as she didn't want to talk about her sister in public. We exchanged phone numbers and addresses.

When someone dies of suicide in most communities, people consider it a shame on the family, brought about by the deceased, and they don't say good things about the person or the family.

The next day, I went to see her. During our discussion about her sister, she said, "My sister was such a beautiful girl, and she was my best friend. I miss her so much. Though she was a couple of years older than me, she humbled herself and fit into my group. We went almost everywhere together. She really didn't have friends her age; she was always with me and my friends. She was a big sister to me in so many ways and was very protective of me. My friends and I used to call her 'Mama' and 'bodyguard' in a joking way. She was not old enough to be our mother, but she was very gentle and behaved as a real grown woman, while I sometimes acted my age, as kids will be kids. She sometimes pulled away from some of the games my friends and I played, and she sometimes pulled me out too, as she considered such games dangerous and did not want to be blamed by our parents if anything bad happened to me due to such games.

"She always reminded everyone when to stop playing and when to go to our individual homes. She was more mature than most children her age because she was always with Mom, helping her to care for our siblings. She helped her in the kitchen and was also in the company of other mature adults with Mom sometimes. While I was at school, she was in the farm, helping our father, or at home, helping our mom in the kitchen.

"She finished primary school two years ahead of me. Like most girls in the villages then, our father denied her education and refused to send her to a higher institution. She didn't seem to be bothered by Father's decision not to send her to school. She was content and appreciative of whatever she got. She had planned to marry a young, strong farmer in the village. Her dream was cut short when our father forced her to marry a stranger.

"Our father saw her one day, talking with a boy. My father suspected she was having feelings for the boy, and he warned her seriously about chatting with the boy. Even though she denied having anything to do with the boy, my father did not believe her.

"A few weeks after that, my sister was kidnapped in her sleep in the middle of the night and taken to a man's house in the next village; a man she had never met and one who was about forty years older than her.

"A few months following her forced marriage, she committed suicide by jumping into a well full of water and drowned at the back of her so-called husband's house. She could no longer bear the brutality of the man she never wanted to marry. My parents and some elders in the community blamed her for committing suicide and said she brought shame and humiliation to their family.

"From the day my sister was forced to marry that man that was old enough to be her father, who also had another wife and children, she became a punching bag to the man. He beat her up over little things; not doing house chores, not participating in his family activities, and refusing to have sex with him. The man had to seek help from two of his friends who held her down each time he made love to her because she never consented to having sex with him. From the day she died, part of me died with her. I became very much afraid of my life too, as my parents, who were not remorseful about my sister's death, may also force me to marry one day. Soon after the death of my sister, I ran away to the city and worked as a servant for a hotel owner, where I met my husband a few years later. Even after the death of my sister, my parents still claimed they did the right thing."

This did not have to happen. These parents had no remorse over their daughter's death and no change of heart. Society regards this as normal, and nothing ever happened to her husband or her parent.

Those who kill their daughters and wives in the name of culture and honor have ready excuses, such as:

- She refused to wear traditional wear
- She refused to stay in a forced marriage
- She refused to have sex with her husband
- She has engaged in homosexuality
- She was a victim of rape
- The law of their country permits it
- It's a religious practice
- She befriended a boy outside of her culture
- She was pregnant out of wedlock
- She had committed adultery
- She had started dating and having sex before marriage
- She had cheated on her husband (or he suspects it)
- She practiced cultures other than her own
- She wanted to leave her husband
- She wanted to choose her own husband
- She had disobeyed her parents

Other civilized countries, like Canada, are not left out of such crimes committed by immigrants. Much domestic violence has recently made the headlines in Canada.

In Canada, large numbers of immigrants who migrate from all over the world came with their traditional and cultural beliefs. Most people are able to practice their cultural beliefs as far as it is within the law. But certainly honor-killing is not accepted in Canada. Regardless, many still think they can get away with honor-killing here in Canada and other parts of the civilized world. There has been lot of crimes committed by immigrants who believe in honor-killing, and many of these crimes ended up in senseless killings.

Over the years, here in Canada, many crimes had taken place in the name of honor. This includes fathers in some communities killing their daughters in the name of honor. Some of these killings are as a result of suspicions and belief that their children are disobeying them or behaving like Westerners.

A girl can be killed for not staying with the husband of a forced marriage and for living like the citizen of the country where she lives. When someone is killed in honor, family members don't talk about it; they keep it as a big secret. Some men kill their wives due to lack of love. Some men are not ready to marry, but they do so to honor their parents. Some men from this culture and from other African countries marry for some of the following reasons other than love:

- To avoid shame
- For control
- To promote their cultural values
- For social reasons
- To be accepted in the community
- Because they are getting old
- To please their father or parent
- To have children
- Family and societal pressure
- Because others are married
- Because that is what people do when they grow up
- Because they believe the woman will solve their problems by doing everything for them

Men who believe that their problems will be solved when they get married should think again, because problems do not just go away because you are married. Marriage may complicate your problems if you are not responsible. Marriage has ups and downs, but if you keep to your vow of "for better or for worse," through good times and bad times, your marriage may survive. Because people of forced marriages do not have the time to make any vows, they have nothing to keep the marriage positive. Women are under the control of their husbands, and such marriages are always unhealthy.

CHAPTER 21

The "Stick" and Circumcision

The "stick" is an old tradition which is still practiced in some rural communities in some Africa countries; it was more common in the Middle East. This is where a girl may be killed by her father or the elders of the community a few hours before her wedding if she is found not to be a virgin during the "stick" test. This test involves a girl's father, mother, or an elderly woman in the family sticking a finger into the girl's vagina the night before her wedding (the finger is covered with a piece of white cloth) to prove her virginity. It sometimes involved one elder member of the girl's husband's family. The stick test is done the night before her wedding, as they believe that if the stick is done long before the marriage, the girl may have sex before her wedding. In some communities, white bed sheets are used to collect the blood. If the girl is a virgin, she would bleed; the father would use the white cloth or white sheet to collect the blood. Her father would present the cloth during the wedding ceremony.

The father does this just before the wedding day to prevent the daughter from having sexual intercourse with any other man before her wedding. Her father would keep the piece of cloth with the bloodstain as long as he lives or as long as his daughter remains married.

However, if the test proves that the girl is not a virgin, her father would consider that the girl has brought shame to his family. The husband-to-be would refuse to marry her, and her father would hand her over to the elders of the community. They would stone her to death or kill her in whichever way they wanted in front of her father's house to clean the shame.

The reason her father keeps the bloodstained cloth is for him to use as proof of the daughter's virginity. If at any time during her marriage, the husband accuses her of not being a virgin before her marriage, as a reason to divorce her, the cloth will then be presented as a proof of her virginity.

> Suppose a man marries a girl and later he decides he doesn't want her. So he makes up false charges against her, accusing her of not being a virgin when they got married. If this happens, the girl's parents are to take the blood-stained cloth that proves the girl was a virgin, and they are to show it in court to the town leaders. The girl's father will say to them, "I gave my daughter to this man in marriage, and now he doesn't want her. He has made false charges against her, saying that she was not a virgin when he married her. But here is a proof that my daughter was a virgin; look at the bloodstains on the wedding sheet!" (Deuteronomy 22:13–20)

Then the town leaders are to take the husband and beat him. They are also to fine him a hundred pieces of silver and give the money to the girl's father. The money is to be given to the girl's father because the man has brought disgrace on the girl. However, she will continue to be his wife, and he can never divorce her as long as he lives.

But if the allegation is true, and there is no proof that the girl was a virgin, then they are to take her out to the entrance of her father's house, where the men of the city are to stone her to death. She has done a shameful thing among our people by having intercourse before she was married, while she was still in her father's house. In that way, you will get rid of the evil.

Fathers who practice this act justify their practices as an act that has been approved by God because it is in the Bible.

Circumcision/Female Genital Mutilation

Another way parents inflict pain or punishment on their daughters in some parts of Africa is through circumcision. They circumcise their daughters (removal of sensitive flesh in the vagina), and stitches are made in some cultures to prevent sexual intercourse. These practices sometimes lead to the death of their daughters. The practice is done in girls, sometimes when they are babies. Female circumcision was not mentioned in the Bible, but male circumcision was.

Each one of you must be circumcised, and this will be a physical sign to show that my covenant with you is everlasting. Any male who has not been circumcised will no longer be considered one of my people, because he has not kept the covenant with me" (Genesis 17:13–14). Circumcision was practiced by Jews, Christians, nonbelievers, and Muslims in the ancient time. It was more common in Muslim communities to reduce female sexual desire.

Female circumcision was not peculiar to African cultures in the beginning; it was also practiced in civilized countries. But later on, the practices in civilized countries and some parts of Africa was outlawed. In other parts of Africa, the practice remained a strong part of their tradition, "unchangeable and unchallenged." Even though it is illegal now in some Africa countries, it is still openly and secretly practiced in some communities within the country that outlaws it.

Circumcision and stitching is locally performed by traditional surgeons who are mostly women. It could be done by the mother of the girl in rare cases or by other elderly members of the family. Whoever is chosen to perform the surgery uses local material to do it.

This is the method in which they remove a girl's sensitive part of her vagina. The opening in the vagina is made very small by stitching to discourage intercourse before marriage, leaving enough opening for menstruation to pass through. The vagina remains stitched until her wedding night. In this culture, men are forbidden to have sexual intercourse with uncircumcised girls.

Circumcision for girls is a harmful practice; some girls have died during the process due to excessive bleeding and infection. The procedure is done out of the hospital with unsterilized equipment, like dull knives, thread, razors and scissors to perform the local surgery.

Cutting or tearing open of the stitches occurs fully or partially when a woman with stitches has intercourse. In many Africa cultures, only a husband can tear open his bride through intercourse. A woman's stitches can also be torn open with a sharp instrument if the husband is unable to penetrate or if the husband permits a midwife, traditional surgeon, or relative to do it. Once a virgin's stitches are opened, they cannot be stitched back.

However, restitching of a woman's vagina is practiced in few African countries. After widowhood, if a young widow plans to remarry, the restitching is performed. This is to make sure that the woman does not have intercourse with another man until she gets married again. If and when she marries again, the circle is made fresh.

Circumcising females and stitching of the vagina is considered normal to some African communities, just as is men's circumcision in North America and all over the world. Even though many girls have died during circumcision, parents choose female circumcision over their children's lives.

Circumcision is not always followed by stitching of the vagina in some parts of Africa. Some parents in West Africa circumcise their female children without stitching. They surgically remove the external sensitive flesh of the vagina, after which the wound is left to heal naturally. This does not affect the size or opening of the vagina, but the girl is expected to remain a virgin until her wedding day. Some parents wait until a few weeks into their daughter's marriage before circumcising their daughters in some cultures.

Some women in this culture are unwilling to circumcise and stitch their daughters' vaginas. These women do not believe in it, but because they are in the country where this is a tradition and because they are under the influence of the men, they have to do it. If a woman refuses to obey the traditional practices or goes against the community in which circumcision is practiced, she may be putting herself and her daughter in danger. In a country where women have no say, refusal may mean a death sentence. Stitches can only be removed without punishment for medical reasons.

Female Genital Mutilation

Practice of female genital mutilation, which is another form of violence against babies, girls, and women in most African countries, has just been banned in Nigeria. This is great welcome news for all women and great news for women's groups who fought endlessly for so many years for the ban of this barbaric act. This is a wicked traditional practice that started many years back, meant to disable women sexually. Any girl or woman who has had her genitals mutilated does not enjoy sexual intercourse or are not as easily turned on as women with their genitals intact. This is one of many practices to reduce a women's power, even during sexual intercourse. Men are circumcised, but it does not affect men the same way as women; it in fact helps men to reduce infection.

Men's sexual feelings are just the same and even better following circumcision. It does the opposite to women; it kills women's sexual feelings and sometimes creates infection and excessive bleeding. In some cases, it leads to major health problems or even death. It leads to sexual disabilities in women (reduction in sexual desire, if any). Many men use those women who have been circumcised to their advantage. Remember that in most cultures in Africa, women have no say over things, not even over their own bodies. They do things when told and have sex when told. Men in these cultures force their women to have sex with them when they want, whether the women want it or not. They use their wives as sex machines and baby-making machines. I heard a man tell his wife that she should submit to him whenever he wanted sex. He said her feelings during lovemaking were not important, but his were.

However, there are some loving husbands who would put their wives in a romantic mood before having sex with her, knowing that it sometimes takes longer for a circumcised woman to get in the mood of having sex. Many African women do not know the pleasure of love making as they are forced to make love all the time. They are deprived of the ability to enjoy sex before they even dream of experiencing it. As African women are taught and brought up to serve and please their husbands, they also learn to keep their sexual desire to themselves. Women never ask their husbands to make love to them; they wait until they are asked. Only in recent days are women bold enough to ask their husbands for sex in some African countries; in other parts, it is still a taboo.

The most important thing about the ban on female genital mutilation is that the sharp and dull razor blades of the traditional surgeons will be laid to rest for good. I hope the news goes all over the country, including the rural areas. This is the beginning of women's sexual freedom in Nigeria. I hope other things, like forced marriages and polygamy, will also be outlawed. Mostly, I hope other Africa countries that practice female genital mutilation will learn from Nigeria's example and do the same. Education also played a part in the ban on women's circumcision in Nigeria.

Culture and Religion Control

Men in some cultures use their cultures and religion to control their daughters; in some cases, they have killed them in the name of honor, disowned them, or sold them to older men. Many do not believe in education for women, as they see this as giving power to women and taking power of control away from men. A recent example is the case of the Islamic extremist group Boko Haram, which believes that their religion, which is against women's education, is the only way. This group believes in lack of education for girls and women; some also believe that a girl should be her husband's servant, slave, and baby machine. They want to impose the same beliefs on everyone around them.

Boko Haram kidnapped almost three hundred girls from their sleep in a school in the northern part of Nigeria in March 2014. Another eight girls were taken in the first week of May, and they killed over 150 people in Boronu State by bombing and have committed other criminal acts since then. They also bombed several markets and large gathering groups in Jos, Kano, Abuja, and other villages, which killed several people, mostly market women, to prove a point to the girls' families and to the whole country that they should not educate their daughters. They also believe in early marriage and want everyone in the country to marry their daughters early.

These girls and their parents did nothing wrong. The girls went to school to be educated, like many girls in the civilized world. Boko Haram, who dressed in army uniforms during the kidnapping, told the girls that they had come to rescue them from Boko Haram, the enemy. The girls were told that the Boko Haram group was coming to kill them all. The girls quickly got up from their sleep and hurried into the waiting trucks and were driven away.

On their way to the unknown destination, they realized that they were kidnapped by Boko Haran and feared for their lives. At this point, some of the girls jumped out of the moving trucks, with light to severe injuries, but for others, it was too late. They were taken to unknown destinations.

About three weeks after they were kidnapped, a Boko Haram leader produced a video that was seen throughout the world. He was seen boasting about the kidnapping of these girls and sent this message to the parents of the girls while he dressed the girls in Muslim attire. He said he was converting them to be Muslims. He also said, "I abducted your girls. They are slaves. I will sell them in the market. Western education is forbidden."

The question is, how forbidden is Western education to these groups when they are using some Western technologies, including guns, phones, and ammunition, and some want so badly to send their children to the Western world for a better life? Some of their actions may be due to upbringing and bad traditional influence and lack of responsibility from their fathers.

CHAPTER 22

What Fathers Are to Expect in Parenting

Having children is one thing; raising them well, having a good relationship, and being a responsible father, is another thing. Due to lack of responsibility, polygamy, failure to provide education for their children, especially their daughters, and some fathers having more children than they can care for, there is an increasing poverty level among their children. Millions of children are uneducated in most African countries. They are working as domestic servants, hookers, beggars, traffickers in the sex industry, or drug dealers or commit armed robberies and kidnapping. There are boys in the sex trade as well, but they are in fewer numbers. Many children are without access to basic health care, welfare, and social services

Many children die at a young age due to lack of basic care and neglect from their parents. Some men boast openly of how many children they have and focus on the quantity instead of the quality of life they should provide for their children. In some poor counties in Africa, children sell things on the roadside. Some are hooking in the middle of the road in between cars and are sleeping under bridges, with no home to call their own. Some of them die helplessly on a daily basis from the most common infection that could be prevented or treated with simple medication, which their parents are unable to afford.

Due to lack of understanding and illiteracy, the poor keep having children without thinking of how to provide them with quality lives. If one child dies due to poverty and lack of care, they replace that child with another.

They believe that God gives and God takes, and that God will take care of their children for them. They have forgotten the saying that "God helps those who help themselves." God is not going to come down and do things for you unless you make an effort and ask for help.

Poverty is a disease that can be prevented and cured with education. Fathers need to be responsible in order to show their children to be responsible. You should have the number of children you can care for. Raising children is not a game, and your children should not be part of your business deals.

As a father, you should expect the ups and downs of raising your children and handle them as a man. Your children are not always going to be cheap to care for, as you may expect. And they may not be gentle in their ways of doing things, as you would expect, but if you are prepared and have an open mind toward parenting, you will mostly have success. When planning to move your family to other countries, you should expect that your family, especially your children, will adapt to the culture of the country. They will not behave the way you may expect or behave in a way that promotes your culture all the time. Have an open mind; a free mind is a peaceful mind.

If you have an open mind and blend your culture with the culture of the new country, it will work for all involved. Expecting them to follow your tradition 100 percent when you are away from home may set you up for failure in achieving your goals.

Don't let your anger or rigid traditions determine how you treat or discipline your children. The Bible says, "If you become angry, do not let your anger lead you into sin, and do not stay angry all day" (Ephesians 4:26). A father who beats and hurts his children or wife for no reason, or because he may be angry, is committing a sin. He must stop and ask for forgiveness from God and from his family. Do not bring your children up with anger; bring them up with love and respect, and respect will come to them freely if you give it freely. Do not demand respect from your children without showing them respect. If you treat your children, wife, and other people with respect, they will respect you and others because that is what they learn from you.

When a father or parent demands respect from children and does not teach them, the children may be resentful and fearful. Some children walk on egg shells around their father because they don't know when he will get angry and hit them or yell at them unnecessarily. Your children don't have to be afraid of you; they can be your best friends. Bring them up in a Christian way so they can only have the fear of God and respect for you.

Praise Your Children.

The Bible teaches you not to only condemn but to praise. Praise your children when they deserve to be praised; they will appreciate your effort. Children that grow up being criticized learn to condemn and criticize others. Reward them for their good behavior instead of only pointing out the negatives in what they do. Do not use your power as the head of the house to abuse and control your children and wife, just because they have no power to fight back. Show them love, and they will show others love. They will promote your image at home and to outsiders as well. When you smile, the whole world smiles with you! You notice sometimes when you go out in public and smile at a stranger that the stranger smiles back at you. As you give a smile, you get back a smile. You will also get respect back if you give it.

Respect is not hard to give; it is simply an act of kindness and politeness. It also means:

- Paying positive attention to each other
- Being nonjudgmental
- Not bullying others
- Not teasing people
- Being considerate
- Not calling names
- Not making fun of people
- Showing appreciation
- Not discriminating
- Treating other people the way you would like to be treated
- Being friendly
- Accepting people for who they are

Honor Your Father and Mother

Showing respect is not only peculiar to adults; children can also show respect to their parents and other people around them. The Bible asks that children honor their father and mother.

As the Bible says, "Pay attention to what your father and mother tell you. Their teachings will improve your character as a handsome turban or necklace improves your appearance" (Proverbs 1:8–9).

Be polite when speaking to your parents and other people.

Don't be rude when asking for something.

Be considerate to your parents and others.

Pay attention to your parents' rules of the house and respect their culture and traditions.

Be appreciative of what your parents are doing for you.

Always say please and thank you.

Your parents' rules may appear strict to you, but they are made to protect you. Rules are not written in stone, however, so if you feel your parents' rules are too strict, you can discuss it with your parents. They may consider making it less strict to benefit you and them.

Honoring your parent means showing them respect and appreciation and obeying them. It is written in the Bible, "Children obey, your parents in the Lord, so that it may be well with you, so that you may live long on earth" (Exodus 20:12).

- Do not commit murder
- Do not steal
- Do not accuse anyone falsely
- Do not desire another man's house; do not desire his wife, his slaves, his cattle, his donkeys, or anything else that he owns
- Be content with what your parents give you

"A wise son pays attention when his father corrects him, but an arrogant person never admits he is wrong" (Proverbs 13:1).

"My son, if you become wise, I will be very happy. I will be proud when I hear you speak wisdom" (Proverbs 23:15).

"Children, it is your duty to obey your parent, for this is the right thing to do" (Ephesians 6:1). "Respect your father and mother" is the first commandment that has a promise added.

"Children, it is your Christian duty to obey your parents always for that is what pleases God" (Colossians 3:20).

What does it mean to honor your father and mother? It means you should try not to argue with your father and mother. You cannot win a fight or argument with your parents.

To avoid fights or arguments with your parent, stay out of trouble. Remember that bad behavior or wrongdoing has consequences. If you do something wrong to your parents, apologize to them and work towards changing your behavior.

Show your love to your parents by kind words and actions. Be good in school (this means staying out of trouble and getting good grades).

Spend quality time with your parents; this is a way to show them love and to get to know them better.

Ask for what you want politely; do not take what does not belong to you.

Respect and follow the example of your good father. For what your father has done for you, he deserves your respect. "Father is a son's best friend". This relates to a good father, as in the poem below.

What Is a Father?

A father is your God-chosen friend
He loves you even before he sees you
He is your friend in need
He has always been there for you
He always supports you in all you do
He was proud to see you the day you were born
He held you with love even when you were so fragile
He was sad to see you cry, as he was not sure what to do

He was your best teacher even before you started school
He teaches you most of the things you know
His loves you with all his heart
His love for you is without end
He works endlessly to care for you
He put his dreams on hold so you can accomplish yours
He paid your bills for many years
He asks nothing of you but respect and good behavior
He made it possible for you to be where you are

We cannot talk about a good father's affection to his children without mentioning the true and unconditional love a good mother has for her children. There is a saying that "mother knows best." Mother is a friend from heaven. No one on earth can compete with mother's love; it is tender and true. There is no other love so faithful and understanding than that of a mother. It is the only love that starts the same and remains the same forever.

What Is a Mother?

A mother is so many things
She is gentle, kind, and nurturing
With a special touch to everything she does

Talk about a father could last few days but
Talk about mother is endless
True love starts with your mother
Some history of your life starts with your father
Every history about your life starts with your mother
Because she was there from the start
There would be no you without your mother
Mother kept you safe, showed you love and guided you
until you were able to protect yourself
Even after you grow up, she still worries about you
Her worries about you never end
Even after you move far away from home, she feels the
same about you
You are always close to her heart

Respect is all your parent needs from you
Disrespecting them is like biting a finger that fed you
Everything may fade away with time
But your parent's love for you never fades
No matter how old you are, you still are your parent's baby
because you can never outgrow your parent
Just as the moon cannot outshine the sun

What are some other things about mothers?

A mother is the foundation of your life.
She does things for you without complaining.
She stood by you through thick and thin.
She was not scared to hold you, even when you were so fragile.
She had uncountable sleepless nights when you could not sleep.
She worked endlessly to keep you safe without expecting a payment.

She loves you unconditionally.
She is your protector and your best friend.
She made time for you when others had no time.
Her heart breaks when you are hurt.
She has been your best friend from when you were born.
She sacrifices so much for you, just to make sure you are happy.
She fed you when you were hungry.
She is not just a mother but a precious gift from God.
She takes the hard work of raising you as fun.
She always sees you as perfect, no matter how others see you.
She takes you to the doctor when you are sick.
She sacrifices her today for your tomorrow.
No love ever existed like the unconditional love of a mother.

In everything your parents have done for you, all they want from you is respect and kindness.

To be respectful goes a long way to gladden your parent's heart. Some people put more effort in rudeness than politeness. There is a good reword in politeness, so why don't you go the easy way? Be polite. Start with simple things like saying a proper good night to your parents and siblings when going to bed. Say good morning when you wake up in the morning, and most of all, thank God for watching over you throughout the night when you were unaware of your surroundings. And also pray that God guides you, your parents, and your siblings through the day, as you have no control of what goes on out there. Be honest with your parents, and they will trust you

Don't be upset when your parents show concern about you and want to know your whereabouts. It is because they care about you. You may feel you are old enough and independent, but remember that you will always be your parents' baby. Also remember that they mean well for you and want the best for you.

Don't play tricks on your parents, as some of the tricks you are playing today your parent may have played when they were young, so they can easily catch you on it.

Be of good behavior, and it will be well with you.

Do not compare your parents with other parents because they are unique people.

Once an adult; twice a child. Treat your parents with tender care when they are old, just as you would like your children to treat you in your old age. Pay attention to what you learn from your parents, so you can promote their good image outside.

For example, I knew a girl in school in my early years. The girl was always happy, smiling, and jovial. She affected people around her with her happiness. I used to wonder what her secret was for being happy all the time. One day there was a concert in the school. All parents were invited, so her parents came with her. Her father and mother needed no introduction; their smiles gave them away. Everyone knew right away that she was taught a positive attitude from her parents, especially her mother, who was very polite, appreciative, and thankful.

Teachers commended her parents for raising such a wonderful and well-behaved girl. Her smiles also put smiles on other people's faces all the time. Be good, and goodness will follow your all the time.

It is easy to be of good behavior if you get good guidance from your parents, like the example above. But if you did not get a good example from your parents, you can still get it by working hard at it. Children sometimes blame their bad attitude on their parents, for not having a good upbringing. They do nothing to help themselves. It is easy for children who did not do well to blame their failure on their parents, guidance, or upbringing. In some cases, this is not true. There are some children who fail to learn a good lesson taught by their parents. Some pick up bad behavior from their peers, or they join bad gangs and copy self-destructive behavior, as they see this as the easy way out. It is evidence in some cases that your parents tried to guide you in the right direction and failed, due to your disobedience. You may have refused to take directions from your parents when they tried to teach you. In this case, you cannot blame your parents but yourself for not following the directions of your parents. It is easier for some people to blame than to give credit. If you are one of those that refused directions from your parents, and this led to your failure in life, stop the blaming, and try your very best to make things right. It is never too late.

Things will work better for you if you do the following:

- Stop the blaming
- Set a goal for yourself
- Work hard to achieve your goal

Create a life you want to enjoy and live and do it sooner than later. The longer you grieve over your past and do nothing to help yourself, the more life passes you by. Life waits for no one.

Your anger over what happened to you in the past cannot change your today. Start helping yourself, for God helps those who help themselves.

You may be down today but can be up tomorrow if you make an effort. A downfall of a man is not the end of his life. You can't change your parents into who you want them to be, but you can change yourself into who you want to be. Your parents may have made a mistake. You have to forgive them because no one is perfect, including you.

If you feel you made a mistake in the past, learn from it and avoid making the same mistake twice.

"The wise avoid making the same mistake twice, but the fool keeps going back."

If you are wise enough to realize your mistake, be wise enough to correct the wrongs.

Act today to help yourself. Tomorrow may be too late.

Act when you are young and able, as "a fool at forty is a fool forever."

Go back to school if you have not finished your schooling. Education has no age limit. Shake off the self-pity, and try to move on. Self-pity has no good result.

Break the bad habits.

Don't constantly think of how people hurt you; instead, think of how you can improve your situation.

Stop giving negative excuses as a reason not to move on.

If you do not let go of the past, you will not have a bright future. The pain of letting go is less than the pain of holding on to the past.

Others have gone through similar situations and moved past it. You can too, if you try.

If you are serious about getting on with your life, get up and do something about it.

As long as you are alive, you need to get up and strive.

No one owes you anything, but you owe yourself something.

Your parents may have discriminated against you. Turn to God because in God's kingdom there is no discrimination.

Turn to the Bible, believe in God, and have faith in Christ. "Life without Christ is crisis."

Have a heart of forgiveness for God forgives us all.

Act now and stop procrastinating, as time waits for no one.

For those of you who failed and disappointed your parents, it is not too late to make things right. Don't wait until it is too late.

I have heard many children make promises after the death of their parents, sometimes at the cemetery, to make a positive change and turn their lives around. To wait until your parents are dead before you make a positive change in your life or before you make your parents proud is a little too late.

Some people believe that the spirits of the dead hear, feel, and see, and they also believe that the dead watch over their loved ones from heaven and protect them. If you believe in spirits of the dead and ghosts, you will know that there is no physical touch or clear communication from the dead. Your communication with the dead would be like one-way traffic. You do the talking, but they don't respond to you as they did when they were alive. Your belief may be true, but no one has gone and come back to prove this. The only one that has proven this is Jesus Christ.

Why wait until your parents are dead before you make them proud of you? Why not make them proud while they are alive, when you can feel them and hear them tell you how proud they are of you and how much they appreciate your effort? You can do this by believing in yourself.

Believe in yourself and you will be proud of the man you will become.

There may be times when you wish you would have gotten the teaching earlier from your parents and wish your father was there for you.

You may have missed a few years of wisdom, but be hopeful about the future, and believe for better tomorrow.

All it takes is hard work, dedication, patience, and obedience to succeed.

Keep the faith, and you will become the man you have wanted to be.

Grow past your anger so you can have a bright future.

Fathers: Your behavior and rigid tradition may have set your son back in life. If this is the case, it is not too late to change. Be close to your children, and treat their mother with respect. Work with your children to make a difference in their lives.

Be a flexible father.

Fathers that practice rigid traditional rules have to be flexible if they want good results in raising their children in these modern days. Be prepared to adjust to the modern ways of doing things. Don't think that change only affects young people and that they are the ones who need to change their attitudes. This thinking may interfere with your good parenting because changes are for the young and the old; children and parents alike. Flexibility will help to achieve your goal. Be flexible and ready to adjust in order to not put too much stress on yourself and not harm your children in the process. As a father, you must be prepared to change with time. Just as you adjust to the new environment and technology, so you must do the same in raising your children.

Children growing up in this generation do things differently than the way your generation did. Teaching your children about your culture and traditions and disciplining your children must be done in a way that gets your message through to them without harm. There are many options that may be helpful to you in raising your children successfully today. For example, there are counselors and books that can help you if you are not sure of what to do, although a book written on other people's success with children may not be all you need. As every child is unique, so is his/her needs; but a book will give you some ideas or suggest ways to handle different and difficult situations in raising children, which were not available in your day.

Try to understand the changes in technology that affect everyone today, including your children. With understanding, you will find it easy to cope and adjust to the present situation. Holding on to your old, rigid ways of doing things may sometimes cause distraction in the new generation. Some fathers believe that their children have to be the only ones to adjust to their rigid rules and cultural practices, which is the only way they are used to doing things. Anything out of their belief is abnormal and uncomfortable for them. Fathers have to remember that parents also make mistakes. Mistakes are not just for children. If you admit your mistakes, you can learn from them, just like children do.

CHAPTER 24

The Interviews

I had the opportunity to interview some young women and children who were affected by forced marriages. They were able to express their feelings and how it affected them negatively.

The names and places that appear in the following interviews are not real, but the stories are.

Interview 1

My first interview was with a young woman, about forty years old, from Nigeria. She escaped her father's authoritarian control over her and her siblings when she was unable to bear the pain any longer. She ran away from home (a village near the city) when she was about eighteen years old and went to the city to stay with her boyfriend, who was about twenty-five years old and working in the city. Her parents did not know her whereabouts for the first couple of years. Then she sent a message to her siblings, informing them of her safety but refusing to give them the address where she was staying. She also refused to give details of why she'd run away from home.

She described her eighteen years of living with her parents as hell. She did not make any negative comments about her mom but said, "My poor mother was a victim of circumstance. Mother did not have any input in decisions that were made in the house, even when it affected her directly."

She said that she didn't have a voice until she came to Canada. Her father was authoritarian and wanted everything done his own way. He never considered other people's feelings, including her mother's. When she and her siblings disagreed with their father and questioned him or asked for clarification, he would respond by shouting and sometimes beating them.

If you talked back and asked questions, it was regarded as "undermining his authority." She felt guilty for leaving her siblings behind but felt she needed to help herself first, to be able to help others. In a way, she felt her running away from home helped her siblings as well. Her siblings were in contact with her and said their father changed his attitude toward them and became less "harsh" after she left home. He became more accommodating and lenient toward her siblings because he feared they would run away too unless he changed his way of discipline.

While she lived at home, her father beat her into unconsciousness one day, and she was rushed to a nearby hospital. "After I returned from the hospital," she said, "my father did not say much or show any remorse. Instead, he blamed me for the beating. He told me that it was my fault for what happened because I argued with him. After I recovered fully from the beating, I decided to run away. I was blessed in the sense that my boyfriend was from a rich family. Spending money was not a problem for me. He was able to provide for my needs. The only problem was that I could not continue my education in the city. If I did, sooner or later my father would know where I was. I spent about nine months with my boyfriend, planning how to come to Canada. I had a friend in Canada who told me good things about the country, so I decided to apply for school in Canada. I gained admission into one of the colleges. I paid for a year's school fees and other required payments, and then I came to Canada to further my education and to escape from my father's abuse."

"For a while after I ran away, I felt I was still living under my father's strict and rigid rules and was afraid to speak up for myself. I had those bad memories all the time. It took me several months to adjust to my freedom."

When I asked if she resented her father for the way he treated her and her siblings, she paused for a moment, kissed her teeth with false laughter, and said quietly, "I don't believe that my father is a bad and uncaring father, but I believe that his behavior is connected to his upbringing. My father always told us that he had it ten times worse than we did when he was growing up. I can only imagine what that was like for him."

Children raised in a strict-discipline family often become disciplinarians and authoritarian when they grow up. They believe the best way to correct children's wrongdoings is to physically discipline them the way they were disciplined growing up.

I asked her what her mother's role was and if she tried to defend them when their father was disciplining them harshly. She laughed and said, "Nigeria is a male-dominant culture. When I was growing up, most women had no say or any rights in their husband's house, especially the illiterate women. I knew that my mother did not approve of my father's way of disciplining us, but she could not stop him or change his ways. I know too that she felt our pain each time Father beat us. If she said anything or supported us in any way that father disapproved, he would turn on her and beat her too."

"Silence was always her defense, her best answer to Father. People looking at Mother would think that she easily accepted the way Father was treating us, but we knew she struggled with it but could not do anything about it."

Society considered this a good way to bring up children, and the justice system considered it as a family matter then. There was really no protection for children from abusive parents then. Even now, there is only a little protection and improvement in the way fathers treat their children, especially female children in some cultures.

If children call police on their fathers because of child abuse, their fathers would disown them and would label them as a disgrace to the family.

Society would shame and condemn them. The same goes for the wife, if a wife called the police on her husband. The husband would divorce her, and the society would condemn her as well. If her husband divorced her on this ground, he would most likely send her children with her or keep her children away from her. If the children were kept from her, she would be banned from seeing her children. If her children were sent with her, the father may cut off all support for them, including financial support.

Interview 2

A lady I spoke with from a polygamous family told me how stressful it was to experience such a lifestyle. After she stayed in the marriage for some years, the stress and ill treatment from her husband and co-wife, coupled with the birth of her new baby, overwhelmed her. She became depressed, anxious, and had postpartum depression. Her husband and co-wife used this against her and said she was crazy because of the "evil things" she did to her co-wife.

"They ignored me and refused to seek professional help for me. My husband became ashamed of me and asked that I stay in my room all the time, away from the public eye. He did not want his visitors to see me, as I was always unkempt and became very lean. I could not take care of myself and was not eating well. He was ashamed to discuss my problem with his friends. My baby was in my care partially and in the care of my co-wife most times.

"When the news of my illness got to my parents, they were disappointed with my husband. They sent one of our uncles as soon as possible, and he came and took me home. As soon as I arrived at home, my parents and some trusted elders in the family sought professional help for me. I was placed on medication, and they also followed some traditional cures and rituals. The treatment of modern medication and the traditional rituals worked, and I became well again after many months. My parents then realized that it was a wrong decision to have forced me to marry the man. After the treatment for my depression and some other undiagnosed issues, which may have been caused by stress, I asked my parents to allow me go back to school, and they agreed. In some cases, your parents decide what courses you should take, but in this case, I think they learned their lesson and did not interfere in any of my decision making.

"I graduated as a psychologist and have been working in a hospital. When I am not working in the hospital, I am busy helping young girls and families who do not have a voice to speak up. If they cannot express their feelings outwardly, I refer them to other organizations for support.

"My parents became very proud of me; they apologized for the pain and unhappiness they had caused me by forcing me to marry at my early age and asked me for forgiveness. I told them that they were forgiven. I have moved on and put the past behind me. The truth is I may have forgiven, but I have not forgotten. Something like that stays in your subconscious mind forever. My relationship with my parents became better. They never interfered with any personal decisions I made ever after. This also helped my other siblings who learned from my situation, and their relationships with my father and mother became better too.

"I remarried a man of my choice a couple of years after graduating from the university and had three other children. I have been part of their lives in every way. They love me, and I love them so much. My regret, though, is not being able to be part of my first child's life because his father denied me access. I saw him secretly in his school whenever I visited home and explained to him why I could not get custody of him."

In Nigeria, custody of children goes to their father, even if the father is unfit. A father has the right to give custody of his children to any of his family members if he is unable to care for them, instead of giving them to their mother. In most cases, fathers do not compromise; it is their way or no way. If the child becomes problematic, he blames it on the mother for leaving him or on someone else, even if he is the one that drove their mother away. Nothing is ever his fault.

In most of the civilized world, guardianship of a child is commonly given to the mother, unless the court determines it is for the best interest of the child to reside with the father. In this civilized world, there is no discrimination against women with regards to inheritance rights; over there, it is a different world.

Interview 3

Interviewing people at times is not as easy as it seemed, especially in cultures where women are afraid to speak up. It is even more difficult to get a man to respond to an interview positively, as most do not consider abuse of women to be an important issue. I tried to interview many men but most times the response I got was, "Men have control over their families. It's not a big deal and also marrying more than one wife is not a big deal." But they do not want to hear how their controlling behavior affects their families negatively.

One man did respond. He had this to say:

Q. Why did you marry more than one wife?

A. I married my second wife because she was given to me by my parents, and I could not say no to them.

Q. Are you saying that you accepted a woman because your parents said you should? Was there no love between you and your second wife?

A. I did not say anything about love. All I said was that I did not go to look for a second wife, but I was kind of open to the offer.

Q. Do you have any regrets about your decision to accept a second wife?

A. (He smiled) I have no regrets accepting my parents' wonderful gift, but I must admit, it is not easy coping with two wives and many children. Knowing what I know now, I do not advise my children to have more than one wife and many children. Certainly I will never force or arrange a wife for my children. I agreed with you that it is a precious gift that comes with a precious price.

Q. How do your parents feel now, watching you struggling to keep your family going, morally and financially?

A. It depends on their perspective of struggling. To them, there is nothing wrong with anything or the way I am bringing the children up. I think they believe in quantity and not quality. To them, the more children you have, the better. They are from a different generation; they do not really think the same way you and I think. To them, children are blessings from God. It does not matter whether they are educated or not. Plus, education was not important to them because they were not educated and did not know the value of education. In their day, education was not very important, especially for girls. Things have changed. We now live in the new generation, where education is important, and it costs a hundred times more to bring children up these days than in my day. When accepting my precious gift, I didn't think or consider how much it would cost me to care for our children. I had to ask family members for help to care and pay school fees for some of my children when the going was tough. Couple of my children had to stay with other extended family members as servants for financial assistance.

Q. Do you blame your parents for choosing a second wife for you?

A. I do not blame them; they did what they thought was right at the time. That was their cultural belief and traditional practice. I went along with their plan also.

Q. What message do you have for men planning to marry more than one wife?

A. It is up to individuals to do what they want, but I will advise that they make sure they are man enough, morally and financially able, to care for both wives and children. I must admit, it is not fun.

Q. What is it like to marry more than one wife?

A. As in everything you do, there are advantages and disadvantages. I will not say it is all bad. In fact, marriage is a lesson. It is good and bad, fun and difficult. It's hard to explain it. I was with one wife before I married the second wife, and I know the difference. One thing for sure is that you have a divided mind and divided love, and you have to be able to put up with fights and arguments all the time. There is joy in having many children, if you can afford it. Life is never boring, but there is stress in bringing them up, financially, morally, and physically.

Q. How do your wives and children feel about your situation?

A. They have no choice. As you know, in this society, women have no voice and cannot dictate for their husbands. This is slowly changing, due to Western civilization. I am glad that I still earn my children's respect, in spite of it all.

Q. You said they fight all the time. How often do they fight?

A. They fought all the time at the beginning, especially the first couple of years, both physically and verbally. Then the physical fights became less and less and then stopped altogether, but the verbal argument and nagging never stops. It continues to this day.

Q. How do you live with that?

A. I became kind of used to it after a while, and I am able to tolerate it.

Q. Would you say your children from both wives feel comfortable hearing their moms argue all the time, and do they also fight?

A. They have no choice; they learn to cope with it but occasionally they fight, and when they do, I discipline them.

Q. Do you think your behavior is related to your upbringing?

A. Yes, very much so.

Q. You said that your father married three wives. How much freedom did your mother and her co-wives have?

A. I don't think they had much freedom or any control over anything. My mother and the other wives were not allowed to work outside of the home, and they did not socialize very much with people outside of the family members.

Q. Do you ever wonder how your mother felt about sharing your father with other women and the treatment she got from your father?

A. Yes, I knew that my mother and her co-wives did not get the best treatment from my father. When I asked my mother why she put up with the treatment, she paused for a moment and smiled and then said, " Son, there is so much and so many things I gave up from the day I was forced to marry your father. I had no choice, not even the choice of rejecting your father. Son, I am here and have come a long way. Some of the things I went through and still going through, you may never understand." She was right. I may never understand.

Q. You married two wives. Do you think you are treating them better than your father treated his wives?

A. I think so. I sent some of my daughters to school; my father did not send any of my sisters to school.

Q. Why did your mother support you marrying two wives, considering what your mother went through? Does she realize that your wives might be affected negatively; just the same way she was affected?

A. Women have no control over their children; fathers do. Whatever decision he makes for the family goes, whether good or bad. And my mother may have supported me, as she feels this is the cultural norm. She did not know any better.

After the interview, I offered to send someone to buy him a drink. He smiled and said, "Women do not buy drinks for men in my tradition. Men buy drinks for women because women are not supposed to spend their money on men."

"If you visit in my house, and I cook, would you eat it?" I asked.

He said, "Yes, that is different. If you cook at home, I would assume that you are using the food provided by your husband, so I am not directly eating your food."

"We are in the new generation," I reminded him.

He again smiled and said, "Well, that part does not apply to my generation."

The interview with the man made me realize to what extent some men can control their wives, sometimes without knowing it, and how they take every freedom away from their wives, including religious rights, and make them feel worthless, knowingly and unknowingly.

Religion and Women: In some African countries, a wife is expected to change from her traditions and cultural beliefs and practice her husband's culture, including religion. If the husband is a nonbeliever, she may end up not going to church altogether. She could be influenced by her husband's values. There have been many occasions where religion has come between husband and wife. This is very common in forced marriages. In a normal marriage, with love and good relationship, couples have time to resolve their issues and agree on what will work best for both of them. Sometimes they reach a compromise. The issue of who belongs to what religion becomes less problematic after marriage. A woman forced to marry has no time to resolve her religious differences before she gets married. She did not have the choice, voice, or the chance to express her feelings of what she liked or disliked.

Some in-laws influence the way she worships and where she worships. If she is of a different religion, they may fear that she is going to take their son away from their religion. A woman forced to marry, especially if she is young has no voice at all, she immediately converts to her husband's religion. Even if her husband wants to permit her to continue with her religion, he cannot, as this may mean giving up his right to a woman and may mean losing support from his family and the community. In some cultures, children put more faith in their fathers than in God, even after they grow up.

It is expected that a woman will adapt to her husband's culture and his demands. This is an expectation no matter her age or education in some cultures. This makes most women morally weaker than men, even with religion. Some men function under the influence of their mother and other family members, as they believe the only woman they can respect is their mother. This is also some of the behavior they inherit from their fathers. Culture and tradition is proof of who we are as people, and this grows with us, and we intend to behave according to the traditional upbringing.

Whether we believe it or not, things we first learned at home when we were young stay in our subconscious minds, and we don't even know it's there until, at some point in our lives, something pushes it to the surface.

Religion shouldn't be a problem in a healthy relationship between husband and wife, whether forced marriage or not. Religion has never been a problem in my marriage; we both knew before we got married where our faith was. I was attending church before I got married and continued to attend after I got married. My husband, on the other hand, though a strong believer, only went to church occasionally, and sometimes on special occasions. He prayed at home and was always interested in watching the gospel channels on Sundays. He enjoys worshipping with them on TV for an hour every Sunday and occasionally donates to them. Much later in the marriage, he changed and became a full fresh member of a church.

We both had different views in the area of worship for many years. I liked going to church and worshipping with other church members, and he liked praying at home, until he decided to join the church. We now both attend the same church. My husband is traditional in a way and is always promoting his tradition in healthy ways. He never imposes his tradition on anyone. He believes that culture is culture and religion is religion. When you are traditional, it does not mean you cannot be religious. Some people confuse tradition with idol worshipping, which is not the case.

There are people, though, who believe strongly in tradition and do not know any other way. They find it difficult to accept religion of any kind, especially the idol worshippers. These people do not appreciate anyone or anything that would take tradition away from them. They view church as one of those things. My husband is very open and respects every religion. His acceptance and openness makes me feel comfortable when leaving home for church, even at a time when he doesn't go. What matters most is that we treat each other with respect. We have success in accommodating each other's ways of service. With many, it is not easy to come to a compromise, especially if the woman is weak, and her husband is under the control of his parents and other members of his family.

Parents who control their male children also control their daughters-in-law. If a husband cannot break his cycle of control from his parents, it is most likely that his wife will remain under the control of his parents as well. And because he listens and takes instructions from his parents, even on how to run his marital affairs, it's almost impossible for him to have an open mind about anything his wife says and does.

CHAPTER 25

Fathers' Role in Their Daughters' Lives

Africa society supports male superiority. Men are taught to control women in every way from the time they are young. Males and females have separate rules and treatment from the same parents. Females are taught to be submissive. Even some educated men in this society behave the same way as their parents because of the way they were raised. Some learn not to respect women but feel respect from women is their right. Boys learn to be closer to their fathers and girls to their mothers.

In most cultures in Africa and other parts of the world, male children are believed to be the head of the household when their father dies. Female children are expected to respect their brothers as much as their father, even if the son is younger. For example, if a man has four children and the last is a boy, the other three girls are expected to cater to him. Sometimes, the rules of the house do not apply to him just because he is a boy and the only son. Most parents do not teach their sons responsibility when they are young.

It is culturally believed that the son will someday take over the responsibility of the household when his father dies. In this culture, when the father dies, the male child, especially the first son, is expected to take control of his father's properties and responsibilities. If the son is young at the time of his father's death, the first uncle in the family takes control of the properties and hands them over to the son when he reaches the age of maturity. The uncle would be responsible for raising the son and other children in the family until he passes on all responsibilities to him at the right age. The uncle, who must be from his father's side of the family, never his mother's relative, can also marry his late brother's wife if he wants, where this is a custom. If there are no male children before the father dies, only then will the properties be shared among the daughters, according to their age, where this is applicable.

In some other cultures, daughters are not entitled to anything. When their father dies without a male child, the properties would belong to their father's brothers or uncles or whoever has been choose in the family to be the next of kin. Whoever inherits the properties would also take over dictatorship of the family and represent their father in all aspects. In this culture, denying daughters an inheritance and giving it to the brothers or uncle is their way of keeping the wealth or properties in the family.

They believe that if their wealth is given to their daughters, it will automatically belong to their husbands when they get married, and their maiden name and everything they worked for would be forgotten.

For the sake of having male children to keep their name and wealth when they die, some fathers do anything to have a male child. This include marrying a second or third wife, if possible, or divorcing their wives for no reason other than to marry a younger woman or women to bear a male child. They have forgotten that children are from God, and the choice of children's gender does not belong to women. To divorce a wife for no reason is a sin. "She was your partner, and you have broken your promise to her although you promised before God that you would be with her." Then God made a powerful statement: "I hate when one of you does such a cruel things to his wife" (Malachi 2:14–16). The English version of the Bible clearly stated that God does not take a casual view of marriage. He takes note of how husbands and wives treat each other. For this reason, fathers need to appreciate the children given to them by God, regardless of gender, and be content and treat both equally.

It is possible for a father who expects a baby boy to get angry at his wife when she delivers a girl; he may dislike his baby girl from birth. Some fathers barely play with their daughters the way they do with their sons. They do not interact well or frequently with them. Some behave toward their daughters as if they are strangers. Daughters in this culture face lots of discrimination, lack of respect, inequality, sexism, inferiority, and much more from their fathers, as well as the society. Daughters in these societies are taught to grow up quicker and assume responsibilities of adults, more than their sons. Children should be taught responsibilities in a gradual manner.

Acting like a woman is inborn and is to be considered a gift from God. It starts from when you are a little girl, the same as men, though both boys and girls need good guidance from their parents to encourage these roles. In almost all cultures, girls are taught to act ladylike, to be humble, patient, and obedient, and to serve their husbands when they grow up. On the other hand, boys are taught to be strong, to be in charge of the household, and not to show emotions. They are encouraged not to cry but to be strong. This is the practice of ancient times. Girls were taught to be ideal housewives. Ideal housewives did not have jobs, so it was considered a waste of money to educate girls.

There have been some changes regarding male and female roles in some families in the big cities. Educated parents are now adapting to the Western ways of raising children. It is noticeable that lots of fathers are shifting from the strict culture of their parents in regards to raising female children. The gap in the way family treats their male and female children is gradually closing, and many are now educating their female children. It is believed that the new generation in some cultures will treat their female children better than their parents did. Some uneducated men and women need help and outreach to be able to understand the good qualities in their daughters and the importance of educating them.

Raising children, male or female, is challenging and one of the most difficult things. The decisions you make bringing them up will impact their lives in their later years. Sometimes, their highs and lows in life may depend on the way you bring them up and the amount of time and education you provided for them. Though there are times when you tried your best and gave your children quality lives, your best was not good enough. Some children choose the wrong path in life, due to peer pressure and the environment in which they are brought up. In this case, your children's failures should not be blamed on you. Regardless, as parents, if you don't try your best, the failure rate may be higher than success.

Good parents wonder what they did wrong when their children choose the wrong path. It may not be something you did or didn't do. However, if you notice bad behavior in your children, the best way to deal with this is to be strong and supportive and seek professional help before it is too late.

Some or all the negative behavior may change with time and with support and effort from both parents. Time, patience, and effort are needed to assist these children, as they are struggling within themselves and are not sure what to do. Sometimes they put on bold faces and negative attitudes. Inside the boldness and negative attitudes children display at times, however, they have love and affection, and do not know how to show it. Insecurity may be part of their problem as well. They need you to help them deal with this. It takes some effort and time to understand where they are coming from. Sometimes you may never know. All you can do is support them as best as you can and pray that God shows you ways to help them and that God directs them to the right path in life.

Be a supportive parent, especially a father. Some fathers neglect their children as they pursue their own needs and goals. You bring children into this world; they did not ask to be born. It is only fair to make an effort to guide them in the right path as best as you can, without discrimination.

Gender discrimination is destructive to children; unfortunately, it is widespread. It is more pronounced throughout Asia, the Middle East, and almost all parts of Africa. African countries have many ethnic groups and various cultures and traditional practices. Most groups discriminate against girls and women, though some are slightly better than others.

The situation has deteriorated over the years, and it does not seem to be getting any better in some countries. It is worse in some part of Africa; for example, Chinese have more male children than female due to the high rate of discrimination against female children (abortion based on ultrasound accessibility). In this culture, many people believe in male supremacy. If a wife gets pregnant and is proven by ultrasound that the baby is a girl, the husband may ask his wife to abort the baby. He keeps doing this until she has a baby boy. The reason some gave for doing this was the limitation of having one child per family. Before the use of ultrasound to determine the gender before birth, parents from this culture would kill or give away their baby girls at birth and continue to do so until they had a baby boy. A female child is discriminated against even before she is conceived.

Years ago I attended a marriage ceremony of an Ibo friend in Nigeria. The tradition in this culture and most cultures in Nigeria is that a bride's father and elder members of the community bless a marriage with prayers during the ceremony. The first person to pray was the father of the bride. His prayer was for the bride and bridegroom to have a happy marriage and live together in harmony. The next prayer was for his daughter to multiply in her husband's house, and he prayed continuously for his daughter to have male children for her husband. He said that would carry on the legacy of their family. Not once did he mention a baby girl, and everyone responded loudly, "*Isee*" (amen).

Newlywed couples are made to believe right away that they must have a baby boy. In some cultures, they believe that a woman has no place in her husband's house without having a male child. From the moment the woman enters her husband's house; her highest hope is to have a baby boy for her husband. Some are being pressured to get pregnant right away and give birth to a male child. Pressure starts from her own husband sometimes and other times from her own family and her in-laws.

As mentioned, when a male child is born, he is taught that he is the head of the family, and is told that the inheritance of the family will be passed down to him some day. The right of education is given to him, and he may join in the family business when he grows up. The power of control is given to him. Girls are taught that education is out of reach for them in some communities.

159

It's necessary to break this cycle of gender discrimination so that female children can have equal rights in their parents' houses, in society, and also in their husbands' houses.

Some groups in the country, like ACASA, (Anti-Child Abuse Society of Africa), are raising awareness about different forms of child abuse and are fighting against harmful traditional practices that occur on a daily basis. Child abuse is more common in some parts than others, especially in the rural communities. In this part of the county, fathers force their underage children to marry, some as young as eight years old. Some of the affected children reach puberty in their husband's house. Their parents use extreme violence in some cases to ensure their daughter marries the man they choose for her.

Many of these girls face lots of problems; some suffer "obstructive labor" and as a result, develop fistula (a whole between the vagina and rectum or bladder that is caused by prolonged labor, leaving a woman incontinent of urine or feces or both). When this happens, they are abandoned by their husbands and are driven away. Some of them end up dying from lack of medical care and heartbreak. They have no support from their parents, who believe that the woman has brought shame and bad luck to the family, and they do not want anything to do with her.

CHAPTER 26

Extreme Control over Female Children

E ven living in a civilized city, some parents remain uncivilized and continue to practice their timid social and cultural behavior as if they never left their countries. They expect their children to practice their culture 100 percent, even in another country. If their children refuse to follow in their footsteps and act as they want, they consider this as disobedient and shameful, and this may be enough reason to kill their children. Another reason some parents give for killing their children, especially their daughters, is to avoid being shamed by society. It's more important to them than the lives of their daughters. Some of these girls who were forced to marry knew ahead of time that their parents would force them against their will someday, but they were powerless and could not do anything about it. Some are killed before they could carry out their plans to escape the ugly situation.

Some children of immigrants are caught in the middle of different cultures; the cultures where they were raised and the culture where they emigrated. For some children of immigrants who are born into other cultures, their parents still expect them to act differently from the culture they are born into, even though they know nothing about their parents' culture. The same parents that brought them to civilization also forbid them to act civilized. Some daughters of immigrants have been sent home and forced to marry for going against their parents' wishes, in order to prevent them from marrying people from cultures other than their own.

It would be wise for parents to check out the culture and traditions of the countries to which they want to emigrate, and weigh the pros and cons of the culture, the effect it will have on their children, and how it will impact their traditions as well. If after consideration, they feel the culture is not right for them and their children or unborn children, they should consider staying in their home country.

You cannot bring your children to civilization and expect them to act timidly or live separate lives from the culture you brought them to. If you must immigrate to another country, you must be ready to practice its culture. You should not forget about your culture altogether, but to some extent, you must be respectful of other cultures and must not force your children to practice your culture 100 percent of the time, especially if they are born into other cultures. You can only try your best to encourage them.

Children forced to marry are targets for being killed if they refuse to stay in the marriage. Unfortunately, they are not the only ones facing danger. Anyone who tries to help them can also be a target in some cultures.

An example is that of Malala, a girl who was shot on her way from school in northwestern Pakistan. The Islamist group said it targeted her because she was promoting girls' education and "Western thinking" (in a report by the Associated Press). Malala is one of those fighting hard to save other girls from oppression, abuse, and discrimination. Even after she was shot, she continued fighting to promote what she believes in (equal treatment and opportunities for both boys and girls). She promised to continue the fight, even with her life on the line. May God bless and protect her in her struggle; amen. Please join Malala and many other groups for the fight to liberate girls, to put an end to forced marriages and honor-killings. It will take a girl like Malala and many others to change parents' attitude toward their daughters. It will also take a girl or group of people to put an end to illiteracy and change the way men in the third-world countries treat girls and women. Though Malala and some other organizations are trying their best, they cannot do it alone; they need your help and support to make this a reality. There is strength in numbers. Do you want to help but are not sure how to lend your support? Consider the following:

- You can advocate for girls to be educated in your society
- You can help to build girls' confidence
- You can encourage parents to give their daughters the right to choose their own husbands at the right age
- You can help to create awareness of the girls
- You can report to the authorities if you witness child abuse
- You can encourage the girls affected to speak up
- You can help promote education for girls
- You can pay school fees for the less-privileged girls in your society, if you can afford it
- You can direct affected girls on where to get help; if they are under age, seek help for them
- You can build a school in poor communities, if you can afford it; just like Oprah Winfrey has done in some African countries
- You can help groups and individuals financially to promote awareness about forced marriages

Many people have wondered who these parents are who treat their female children like servants. They are like any other parents, but what goes on in their minds cannot be explained by others. I suspect, however, that something is not right with parents who kill their children in the name of honor. Some people believe that they are normal but do what they do because they have the power and control to do it. There may be other reasons; the following may be some contributing factors:

- They have low self-esteem
- They are controlling
- They are abusive
- They may lack knowledge of how to parent
- They may suffer from mental illness
- They may behave a certain way, based on their upbringing
- They may have grown up in abusive homes themselves, and it is the only way they know
- They may lack self-control
- They may be overly jealous
- They may lack self confidence

- They may be poor and use their daughter for financial gain
- They may lack love
- They may be emotionally unstable
- They may not know God

A parent who abuses a daughter, sells her, forces her to marry, or kills her because of the way she dresses and talks must be suffering from some or all of the above. The unfortunate thing about this is that these children have no support from their mothers. Some mothers do feel their daughters' pains but remain silent or even support their husbands because they fear that speaking up will get them killed or lead to divorce. For these reasons, they stay and suffer in silence.

Women in this culture would prefer to suffer in silence than to put themselves and their children through the agony of broken homes. Broken homes are stigmatized in their society. A woman may feel that everyone would be better off if she obeys and accepts things as they are. Some women do not want their marriages to end in divorce because in some communities, divorce does not only mean leaving your husband; it also means leaving your children behind. These women are so controlled that they forget about their rights, even if they are in the civilized part of the world. They are treated the same way and are afraid to speak up. Every women needs to know her rights and be able to exercise them.

As a woman; old or young, married by choice, by arrangement, or by force, you have the following rights in your marriage:

- You have the right to good treatment from your husband
- You have the right to love and be loved
- You have the right to be trusted by your husband
- You have the right to good care from your husband
- You have the right to not allow your husband to lower your self-esteem
- You have the right to be treated with respect by your husband
- You have the right to be assertive
- You have the right to free movement

- You have the right to disagree with issues that are not comfortable for you
- You have the right to a happy and loving marriage
- You have the right to a healthy marriage
- You have the right to voice your opinion and be heard
- You have the right to make a positive change in your marriage
- You have the right to have your values respected by your husband
- Most importantly, you have the right to report abuse in your marriage

If you are missing any of the above in your marriage, it is considered an unhealthy marriage.

Correction Is Not Abuse

I have raised awareness about men's control and abusive behavior toward their wives and children. I want people, especially women, to understand, however, that there is a difference between correction and abuse.

There will be times in a marriage when a husband and wife will need to correct each other's wrongdoing. A gentle correction from your husband does not necessarily mean abuse. We live in a generation where people are sensitive to lots of things; even jokes, in some cases, are taken as abuse. It is important to recognize the difference.

If your husband corrects your wrongdoing privately, in a proper manner, and asks gently that you not do things that would bring embarrassment to you and to him; this is not abuse. Instead, you can work toward changing your attitude for the better. For example, if a man and his wife went to a party or other outing, and his wife was drunk and said inappropriate things and behaved in unacceptable manner, the husband would have the right to gently correct her behavior in private when they get home, so that such behavior would not be repeated the next time. A wife can also correct her husband in the same manner. You can both correct each other's wrongdoing privately without embarrassment. Gentling correcting each other in private and in the proper manner is part of love.

You can only correct someone you love; you cannot correct your enemy. Correction must be made in moderation. However, correcting someone over every little mistake or in public places to cause him or her embarrassment is abusive. It is always better to correct people with an explanation; explaining the impact his or her behavior could have on others. This is the best way to make your loved one realize his or her behavior was inappropriate. Also, correcting your loved one in private, at the right time, in the right tone of voice, in the right place, and with good intentions, is the best way to get your message across and the best way to get good results. Do not correct people right away if they are drunk or very angry, as this may lead to a fight between you and the person you are trying to correct.

27

Other Interviews

Interview 4

I had the opportunity to interview another young and intelligent lady from another part of Africa, who shared her experience growing up. Her father was legally married to her mother but had another woman and children outside of the marriage.

"He kept his relationship going with the other women while married to my mother. This made him not available at home when we needed him. My mother was educated and smart; she has a college degree and worked outside of the home. Her working outside of the home, though, made it hard for me and my siblings to cope sometimes. There are times when you need both parents with you in the house or one at home all the time, but this was never the case, though we had a helper who came in the day to watch over us and helped to do the cleaning in the house. We could not relate to her as our parent; she was an older lady, uneducated, and spoke little English. This made it impossible for her to assist us with our homework or answer any questions relating to homework. I became my sibling's caregiver and sitter when my parents were at work or went out. I basically did everything that was needed at home on the days the helper was off."

She also mentioned that her father was authoritarian and strict. "He would discipline us over the slightest thing. He expected us to be perfect at our young ages. He even punished us for looking directly in his eyes when he was talking to us, as he regarded this as a lack of respect."

When I asked her the part her mom played in stopping her father from abusing them, she had this to say: "Mom was unlike some other women. I know that some women would watch in silence and do nothing when their children were being abused by their fathers. My mom stood up to my father and fought for our rights. Our mother could not just stay and watch Father take total control of her life and ours. She interfered when necessary. Whenever Father punished us severely or physically abused us for the very little things, she would talk to Father."

"She fought for us in a civilized way. We did not even realize she was standing up for us at the time. We only got to know it when we were older. Thinking back, we used to hear Mom arguing a lot with Father; sometimes they got loud. When we asked Mom what the argument was about, she would say, 'Children, it is okay. It does not concern you.' Mother said to us later, when we were old enough to understand, that she had to fight hard to stop our father from destroying us emotionally, as well as physically.

"Mom said that what she went through as a child growing up at the hands of her parent was not pleasant. She could not stay back and watch us go though the same thing or even worse. She knew the emotional scars involved in such an unnecessary act they called discipline.'

"My mother was strict too, but Mother did things in a civilized way. If our actions deserved discipline, she would discipline us as well, but she never caused us any physical or emotional harm. She would explain why she had to discipline us, and she did not discipline us for little things. We were much closer to our mom because she was open and listened to us, unlike Father."

"Our father was home maybe two or three hours in the day, just before we went to bed, weekends included. He spent more time out with his other women or socializing with his friends and extended family members. He wanted to control everything and everyone in the little time he spent at home. He would sound like he was home all day, but sometimes he didn't even know half of what went on in the house. We knew that he was hardly there for us; sometimes it felt like we were living with a stranger or without a father. All our school activities were without our father, including graduations."

"I fled from home at the tender age of eighteen in search of my freedom. I would have stayed to enjoy my relationship with Mom and my siblings but with father's abuse, I just couldn't take it anymore. Mom fought for us but could not stop Father from his controlling actions, or perhaps she became tired of the continued fighting with him almost every day. In most cases, a woman does not win a fight between her and her husband. It is a man's world."

"As the first daughter, a lot of responsibilities were placed on me. I became the 'second mother' to my siblings. When my mother was not home, I became the adult in the house and had to do everything expected of a mother. I was good in doing those things and did it because I wanted to help my mother in any way I could. I saw her struggling with just caring for all of us, with little help from Father and doing all the house chores."

"This made me mature quickly and also made me strong, but it stole my childhood away from me. I really never had a good childhood. When my friends were out playing, I was in the house, babysitting my siblings or helping my mother with house chores."

In most African cultures, the first daughter—then and even now, in most families—is expected to help her mother care for her siblings and with house chores.

"I am glad that I ran away. This made my father realize that he could not continue to treat his children like animals just because he had the authority. He knew the other children would run away too if he did not change his attitude toward them. His strict and rigid ways of discipline affected my father's relationship with us, though it was never really there from the beginning. We became afraid when it was time for our father to come home and became upset at the mention of his name. His disciplinary method destroyed the family love for him. Father was all for himself; he didn't care about anyone's feelings. He made decisions that would affect everyone without asking for our input or offering an explanation of why the decisions were made. He expected everyone to go along with it without question."

Interview 5

"My father was married to my mother for a very long time, with five children, before he got involved with two other women and married them. They both had children for him. He put all of us together in the same house. The house was big but not big enough to accommodate everyone comfortably. The children had to share rooms, some three to four in a room, and each woman had her room. It was like living in a boarding school. All together, we were thirteen children in the family."

"My father was a good and caring man when we were young, compared to lots of fathers I know. My siblings and I had a good relationship with him before he married the other wives. After the second wife came, we became like second-class citizens in our own house, and Father started treating our mother as his enemy. He became so different from the father we'd known."

"Father gave his new wife his unconditional love, and he neglected us and our mother in the process. The war between my mother and the second wife started immediately when she arrived. Whenever fights broke out, physically or verbally, my father would side with the second wife as if she was a saint. The tension in the house was so thick you could almost cut it with a knife. The house became too uncomfortable for everyone, including the second wife. Our house became like a courthouse, where elders gathered almost every week to settle fights between mother and the second wife. Whenever the meetings were held, my siblings and I became prisoners in our own home, locked up in our rooms, only hearing Father, Mother, and the second wife yelling while narrating what led to their fight."

"Most times, the elders sided with the second wife, and they blamed my mother for being impatient with the second wife. I heard one of the elders tell my mother, 'You have enjoyed your husband enough. Give a chance to someone else to also enjoy your husband. You should stop your jealousy and mind your own business.' I was so shocked by this. I never thought there was a time limit for a woman to enjoy her husband and then become his enemy. I thought if this is what marriage was all about, it was not worth it."

"My father's second wife did not give us too much trouble. She couldn't have, because some of us were grown enough to stand up for ourselves and stand up to her if she had started anything. Right from the first day when she came to the house, I promised myself not to give her the chance to control me or any of my siblings. She was just a stranger invading our space. The second year into the marriage, she had her first baby boy."

"After she had her baby, our attitude changed toward her. We loved our little baby brother so much, and we didn't want to separate from him or let our dislike of his mother come between us and the little baby. I didn't want to treat him any different from my other siblings, so it was difficult to love our brother and dislike his mother. Our relationship with the second wife then improved. Our mother did not mind our relationship with our brother and his mother. In fact, her own relationship became a little better with the second wife, what you would call a co-wife relationship. It was never a solid one. With co-wives, there is never a good relationship; they only try to coexist."

"My mother kept herself very busy with her business, as she was in the store most of the time. This helped her to develop her independence. My father, the second wife, and my mother began living separate lives, even though they were in the same house. My mother was making her own money and had a separate account, which was uncommon in this community. The second wife did not work or trade because father would not let her, but he would compensate her financially. He would buy her expensive gifts and helped her to care for her extended family and her siblings."

"After the second wife had two to three children, the responsibility of caring for her extended family affected my father, and he cut back a lot. At this time, some of my siblings and I were attending high school and university, and my father became overwhelmed with bills. This put a strain on his monthly income. Even though Father was not financially stable at the time, it did not stop him from looking outside of his marriage for pleasure with other women."

"After three children from the second wife, Father got involved with another woman, Iyawo (not her real name. *Iyawo* is a common name given to a newlywed in Nigeria). Father got her pregnant and later brought her to the house to join with Mother and the second wife. At this time, my mother had retired to her faith, and it seemed no action of my father's bothered her. She would leave for the store in the morning and return very late in the evening, Monday through Saturday. On Sundays, she took us to church. She did not witness most of what went on in the house between Father and the other wives."

"The second wife did not expect that another woman would ever overthrow her in her glory; she thought she was the apple of Father's eye. I overheard her one day during her argument with Father, telling him, 'What a big liar you are. You told me you love me so much, and you will never be with another woman, and you even told me if you had met me before your first wife, you would not have married her. So tell me, how long did you hold up to your lies? Not very long is it?' Father did not say much."

"After hearing what the second wife said to Father, I felt sorry for her and wondered how deceitful men can be. From the time Iyawo moved into the house, there were lots of arguments and fights between her and the second wife; in fact, they fought like cat and rat. Mom was not very involved; she buried herself in her business."

"There became a big separation among everyone, including the children. Our parents were living individual lives and behaved like tenants in their own home, with each woman caring for her own children. Our house once again was like a war zone and like an elder's courthouse."

I asked how her father coped with all that went on in the house. She said, "My father blamed his marrying Iyawo on my mother and the second wife's constant fighting. My father never admitted his mistakes; marrying many wives, having more children than he could care for, and how his decision impacted everyone negatively. He also refused to acknowledge his own inability to cope with things that were happening in the house and how he deprived us of his love and affection. His love for his children became divided; he didn't have much to offer in terms of love and moral support at this time. The strains on his finances become so obvious. He was unable to afford some luxuries he used to enjoy. After paying our school fees, he would have little money left for other things. He was not really a good role model in our lives. He did not show us unity, love, or how to relate to others in a positive way. He was hardly there for us."

"One of my younger brothers became withdrawn and very shy. I think that was due to the fact that Father was never there for him when he was growing up. All that we heard every day was arguments and defensiveness. There were hardly any happy moments. This affected the children, but it affected the women more. The women were hurting but kept their sadness to themselves and pretended to each other that they were okay."

"Father never showed any remorse for creating the unhealthy environment for everyone; he still found time to have his own pleasure, socializing with his friends and extended family members. He would go out and pretend that all was well at home or that he was a pro in managing polygamy. He hardly went anywhere with us and his wives. I think that was because he could not cope with the number of wives and children he had. Taking everyone on an outing would require two vans or more, and he only had one car.'

"I used to just watch other children go to appointments with their fathers or just watched them communicating well with their fathers. School activities, parent/teacher day, and other social functions were always without our father. My mother went with us, and the other wives went with their children, but Father went somewhere else to socialize. He developed an "I don't care" attitude toward everyone.'

"Our father would always put himself first, regardless of what went on in the house. Even when we were sick, he paid little attention to us. It was always individual mothers that took care of their children; Father was only there for financial support. One thing I am grateful for is that Father gave me and some of my siblings an education. He was only able to pay half of his children's school fees before he retired from his job due to old age. He picked up a part-time job after that, but it was not enough to cover his expenses. My mother had to help him financially to pay some bills, including some of our school fees. At this time, our lifestyle changed for the worse. Eating nutritional meals and eating three times a day became a big challenge, and our school fees were paid late every term.'

"When I finished school and started working, I assisted Father and Mother in paying some of my siblings' school fees. In most polygamous families, this is the norm. You become your brother's keeper. Because I was the oldest child in the family, my parents placed so much responsibility on me, financially and morally. As soon as some of my other siblings graduated from the university and started working, they also helped with the responsibility of paying school fees for others. Later on, our parents' responsibilities became fully ours, as they did not have any savings. My father's financial situation became even worse after retiring from his part-time job, as he was getting a small amount of money from his pension, and sometimes his pension money was paid late. Mom sold her store, as she was not able to manage it any longer due to age and stress. It was a big struggle for us but a happy ending, as we all worked together and helped each other through school, and we were all educated."

Interview 6

The interview with this woman was a little different from the others. Her co-wife war and her husband's neglect put her at health risk. This woman was forced into polygamy; she was forced to marry her husband at age seventeen, and the man was about twenty-five years older. The man had four children from his first wife; his older son from the first wife was eighteen years old, so her husband was old enough to be her father.

Her parents married her to her husband because the husband was very kind to her parents and helped them out at times when they were financially in need. She said, "I was given as a gift and in appreciation to my husband. Even though he treated me like garbage, they could not say anything to him or take me back." Tears rolled down her check as she continued her story. "I was treated like a slave in my husband's house. I had no say in whatever went on in the house, and no one showed me love or respect. Everyone treated me like a stranger and an intruder."

"I was so controlled by my husband. I was not allowed to go out and was not allowed visitors. He only allowed the people he knew to visit with me, and it felt like I was in jail. I was doing every household chore, including washing his children's clothes. I ate alone when others sat as a family for their meals. About a year and half later, I had a baby girl. She became my comfort and the only person that made me happy in the house, but the joy the baby brought to my life was not enough to take my pain away completely. I was still suffering in silence."

"When I realized that I had nowhere else to go, I fought back and fought everyone on my way to gain ground and to be recognized as a member of the family I'd been forced into. There were more fights and arguments, and things got worse before they got better. I had to call on the elders sometimes to talk to my husband as well as my co-wife. What hurt me more was my husband's calling me names and referring to my parents as needy and poor. He felt he did me and my parents a big favor by marrying me. After a long fight I gained some kind of recognition, and my baby was regarded as one of the children."

"When I was treated as an outcast, I became very sad and depressed. I had so many thoughts, which included running away, killing my husband, and also killing myself. I thought again that if I put these thoughts into action, none of this would benefit me. If I had killed my husband, the community would have stoned me to death. If I had ran away, I would be caught and brought back to the same husband and face even more punishment. And if I had killed myself, I would have done everyone a favor. My co-wife would be happy, as she would have our husband to herself. My husband would not miss me because he had nothing to lose. He would have married another wife or wives as cheaply as he married me, if he wanted. I realized that if I acted on any of my thoughts, I would have been the biggest loser of all."

"I thought that fighting to remain in the marriage and being recognized in some way was better for me. I gained some recognition after a long fight and was referred to as a member of the family after seven years of marriage. The fight with my co-wife and the disrespect from my husband and his grown children, who felt I was a gold-digger, never stopped, but it got a lot better, to the level of tolerance."

I thanked her for sharing her bitter experience and commended her for her effort to stay alive. Many girls and women who find themselves in a similar situation are unable to fight for themselves or their children. Many act on their evil thoughts and do the wrong things. Death is not a solution to a bitter experience. The dead cannot fight for justice, but the living can. At the time of this writing, she is still married to her husband and coexisting with her co-wife.

Interview 7

This interview is different from the others, but in every story, a female child is always a victim of an attempt by some fathers to get out of an unpleasant situation by using their daughters. This happened in the eastern part of Nigeria a few years back, though I understand that similar things are still happening in that part of the country, even now.

The woman I will call "Hope" is from a rich and well-respected family. When she was growing up, she had a good relationship with her father that lasted until she was in her teens. Her father's obsession to have a male child changed her relationship with him and changed her life forever.

Hope is the eldest of five children, all female. Hope and one of her sisters are from the same mother; the other three children are from a different mother. Hope's father sent her mother packing when Hope was about nine years old and her sister was five because the mother was unable to have a male child for him.

"After my mother had the two of us, she could not have another child. My father became inpatient and put so much pressure on her to get pregnant. When she could not get pregnant on time, my father sent her away. I love my mother so much, and I wanted to go anywhere she went, but my father would not let me and my sister go with her. In this culture, children are not allowed to live with their mothers. They say that children belong to their fathers. Mother visited us regularly for the first year before my father married my stepmother, the mother of my other three sisters."

"I think due to jealousy from our stepmother, the visits from my mother became less frequent. Two years later, my mother married another man, and the visits stopped altogether. She was only able to visit us in our school once in a while."

"In this culture and in most Nigerian cultures, when something goes wrong in a marriage, anything at all, the women are to blame, and that is not right. My father even blamed my mother for her inability to have a male child or for not having other children after us. Married men never do anything wrong, and if he does, it is believed that his wife made him do it. My mother later had two male children for the husband she married after she left my father. On the other hand, my stepmother had three female children for my father."

"Regardless of the fact that my mother was no longer with my father, I was still very close to my father, though things were never the same in the house. His wife tried her best to take good care of us. She was never jealous of my relationship with my father and never tried to separate us, but it was never the same. She commended me for being a good stepdaughter most times. I was very good with her children (my sisters), and I loved them the same way I loved my other sister. I was very respectful to her. The relationship with a step mom, though, is never the same as with your mom, no matter how much your step mom tries."

"In your mind, your mom is always your mom. Just your stepmother's appearance in the house sometimes reminds you that she has taken your mother's position, even though it is not her fault that your mother left. But you still wish it was your mom in the house instead. If you happen to have a bad stepmother, then you are in big trouble."

"Whenever we had parent/teacher day at school and saw the other children together with their parents, I felt a bit low and wished it was my father and mother attending on my behalf. I gave credit to my step mom; she tried her very best to bring us up from where my mom stopped. She was a quiet woman, just a housewife that my father wanted her to be. She did anything my father asked her to do, as most old-fashioned women would. She did not have a say in any decisions that were made in the house."

"When I was almost twenty years old and in the second year at the university, my father called for me one day. I thought it must be something very important because my father never really called for me; he just talked to me whenever he saw me. The only time he talked to us was if any of us had low grades in school, and he reminded us of the importance of education and to let us know how much it was costing him to send us to school. At this time, we were all doing well in school, and it was not exam time, when he constantly reminded us to study hard."

"After dinner, I went to answer my father's call. He was sitting on the loveseat, watching TV. He invited me to sit next to him, and I thought that it must be a serious matter. I didn't see any anger in his face, so I didn't think I was in trouble. I waited to hear what he had to say. He turned off the TV and asked me to put on the second light, as the place was a little dark. I thought he wanted me to read something to him, but his silence was getting to me, so I had to ask, 'Papa, what is it you want to say to me?' He looked up at me and said, 'My daughter, what I am about to ask you is very important to me. It will benefit you and all members of this family. The family's future depends on your acceptance or refusal to do this.' I knew then that it was a serious request."

"He then said, 'Hope, my daughter, you know I love you so much and can do anything for you. You have always been my favorite daughter.' Before I said anything, he looked at me and said, 'My daughter, would you do this for me? Would you do me this favor? Would you take my shame away?' I didn't know that my father had shame to uncover. He had money and was well respected in town. I asked him repeatedly, 'Father, what do you want me to do for you? Name it, Papa. I will do it if I can.' As an obedient daughter and the first daughter in the family, I was always agreeing with my father and did basically anything he wanted me to do for him. I was very responsible in my role as the first child. I was much more responsible than most girls my age; sometimes I took on the role of a male child, just because Papa did not have a son. All I did for Papa was with love and respect."

"'My daughter,' he said, 'I want you to remain in the family house with us.' I quickly answered, 'Papa, I am here. I am not going anywhere any time soon. Remember, Father, that I still have a couple of years more to finish my university education, and I plan to remain here and work after that, so, Papa, don't worry.'"

"He then sat up straight and called out, 'I want you to remain in the family house and bear us a male child that will carry on the legacy of this family. You know that I am getting older, and I do not have a son. If I die, my wealth will go to another person or another family. All my family wealth and inheritance that has been passed down from generation to generation in this family will end with me. I don't want to be the person that will bring down the name of this family.'"

"I looked at my father with shock and disbelief. I was silent for a while, not knowing the right thing to say to Papa. He quietly awaited my answer. Tears started rolling down my face as I looked at him. I raised my voice after a long silence and asked furiously, 'Papa, are you suggesting that I sleep with you to have a male child for you and remain here as one of your wives?' My father answered in a deep, low voice, 'No, my daughter, that is not what I mean. I love you as a daughter. I can never sleep with you.'"

"I was again confused and surprised and doubted if I'd heard him right. Then he said, 'I would want a man to get you pregnant out of wedlock while you remain in the family house. Your son will bear the family name because you are not married, and if I pass away some day, I will have the satisfaction of knowing that my inheritance will be given to my blood family. As long as you remain unmarried, everything would go to your son.'

"I told my father that the conversation needed to end because I could not think of what to say. I said I would give him an answer the next day. Early the next morning, I went to see my father in his apartment. After greeting him, I told him I'd been awake much of the night, trying to think of ways I could please him. I said, 'Papa, I thought about what you asked of me, and I came up with these two suggestions: (1) I would like to wait until I finish my education and then get a man that I love to have a child with him; or (2) you prepare a separate apartment for me and the man in the compound, so I can have some privacy with him when we eventually get married.'

"He stopped me just as I finished my last sentence and said, 'Look, my dear, time is a factor here. I can't wait until you find someone you love, but giving you a separate apartment wouldn't be a problem; only if you do not live in the separate apartment with a man. It will just be for you and your son and your other children.' He looked hard into my eyes and said rudely, 'The message I am trying to tell you is that the baby boy would not have a father involved in his life; otherwise, the purpose would be defeated.' He said this with confidence, as if he knew that my first child would be a boy or as if he knew that I would ever give birth to a baby boy."

"I suspected then that I was in trouble with my father. I had to watch what I said because if I said the wrong thing, my father could get angry at me, and I did not want him to know that I disagreed with him in this sensitive matter. I asked my father to give me more time to think of a better solution. He told me not to keep him waiting much longer. I cried all day and night, not knowing what to do with my life. I had no one to talk to about this. I didn't want my siblings to know about this, as they were too young to understand. It was unfortunate that my mother was not around to share my pain or just to have her shoulder to cry on, even though she would have been powerless to help; at least she would have listened."

"When I got to school the following day, I thought I should share my pain, which was all over my face, with someone. I called to a couple of my friends after the first session and told them what I was going through at home with my father. I expected a negative reaction from them, but to my surprise, they were not surprised at all. One of my friends knew someone who was forced into a similar situation and said that the girl was from a royal family.

"I asked what then happened to the biological father of the child born in a situation like that. One friend explained that the rumor was that the king got one of his servants to sleep with his daughter, and she gave birth to two children, a boy and a girl. After the servant slept with the king's daughter, he was threatened never to say a word to anyone; or he would be killed. The only way for the grandson to be the next king was if there was no father in his life. Rumor also had it that the king's daughter started developing an interest in the servant and was giving him special treatment; the king was not happy about it. He feared that his daughter would someday fall in love with the servant, and his purpose would be defeated."

"The servant suddenly disappeared and never resurfaced. There was a strong suspicion in society and among the other servants that the king killed him, but no one could face the king openly. He might have killed him to cover up his secret deal with the servant. If the servant had not disappeared, maybe the king's secret would have been in the open and would have brought shame to him and his entire family. The king would had lost everything he'd tried to protect."

"I knew then that my life would be in danger if I refused my father's request; he would never forgive me. If I went ahead with his request, I would be putting someone else's life in danger, and my children would never have the opportunity to know or grow up with their biological father. Either way, I was already in trouble and had to find my way out of it. I told a couple of my trusted friends of my plan to run away, and I also expressed my fear of not knowing where to go. Right away, one of them told me that I was not alone in this; they would be behind me in my journey."

"I excused myself from class one afternoon, went to the bank, withdrew all my savings, and then deposited it into my friend's savings account so that my father would not have access to it. I had saved quite a bit of money because my father always gave me more than I needed whenever I asked him for money."

"On getting home that day, I lied to my father and told him that I needed some money to buy school supplies and for my personal needs, which my father gave me right away, with a reminder that he was still waiting for my answer. I promised I would give him an answer soon. Papa was very kind to me; he never questioned when I asked him for money. I took the money to my friend, who put it away for me, until I was sure where I was going. I kept my distance from my father and avoided him as much as I could. I waited for him to approach me again; until then, I did not say anything to him about it. Little by little, I took most of my valuable stuff from the house to my friend's house for safekeeping."

"One morning, when I was on my way to school, my father called to me and asked me why I had not gotten back to him with an answer to his request. I promised to talk to him about it when I returned from school that afternoon. That was the day I left home. I went to school that day and never returned to the house. That night I slept at a friend's house, and she connected me with her friend in the big city. I left for the city the following day to join her friend, who lived with her parents. Her parents were Christians and very nice people. They accepted me after I told them my story. While in the city, I felt safe because it was a very big city. It was not easy to locate anyone who did not want to be found. My siblings were worried to death about me, I heard. They thought something terrible had happened to me. I knew that my father knew that I'd run away and may have told my stepmother, but he did not know where I went."

"For the first two years after I left home, no family members knew where I was, only a couple of my friends from school, and they kept it to themselves.

While in the city, my education was put on hold because I could not afford it. I was very happy that my friend's parents, that I called Uncle and Auntie, took me in after hearing my story, which they also condemned. Uncle was a successful businessman who was financially responsible for everything in the house and paying for their three children's school fees. Auntie was a petty trader who made just enough money for her upkeep. As much as they would have loved to pay for me to continue my education, they could not afford it. The first two years in the city, I helped Auntie in the store, where she sold women's clothing. From her little profit, she would give me some money at the end of the month for my upkeep."

"After two years in the city, I sent a message home to my siblings, informing them that I was alive and safe, somewhere in the big city. I was encouraged to do so by Uncle and Auntie but did not disclose the address. If I had, I feared my father would come after me, and my friends would be in trouble. I didn't want any of this to happen. When I was twenty-three years old, Uncle got me a job with a big company in the city as a receptionist. The salary was not the greatest, but I was very happy, as it gave me the opportunity to meet with different people and talk to people from all over Nigeria and outside of Nigeria. I met my boyfriend, who is now my husband, after six months of working there. He was also working with the company at the time."

"He left for London, England, for further studies a few months after we met. He later wrote to ask me to visit with him, which I did as soon as I could. His invitation was one of the best things that had ever happened to me. It was an invitation to freedom. My visa to travel to London was quick; I was able to afford my plane ticket because I was not paying rent and was not paying for food. Uncle and Auntie were helping me out with that."

"When I got to London I decided to stay, so I lived with my boyfriend in the one room he rented in a rooming house. We both lived a students' life (cheap and low-key) for about four months, and then I got a job as a store assistant, and we moved into a one-bedroom flat. The following year, I enrolled in one of the universities, and I studied counseling and women's affairs. I graduated four years later, and right after my graduation, I got a job working in one of the women's shelters. I married my boyfriend right after that, and we now have two children together."

"I went home for a surprise visit after ten years in London. I heard my father was worried about me while I was away and blamed himself for my leaving his home. While away, I communicated with my siblings but never asked after my father; I didn't care how he was doing. I knew that my siblings told him of my communication with them and told him that I did not want to communicate with him."

"I stayed in a hotel when I arrived with my children, ages five and three. My husband could not go with us due to his busy schedule at work. I sent for my siblings as soon as I got to the hotel. In a few minutes, the hotel lobby was packed with my visitors. I was happy to see all of them. My immediate junior sister was married a year prior but no children yet; her husband also came with her. They visited for a couple of hours, and just before they left, one of my sisters asked if she could tell my father about my visit. I agreed. I knew that my father could not force me to do anything I did not want to do. If he tried anything, I would have reported him to the authorities."

"I had my education and would not be a pushover. I had my passport and ticket to go back when I wanted. I told my children that Grandpa would come to visit with us; they were excited. I did not talk to them much about my father before our visit, but I told them several times that my father was in Nigeria. To my greatest surprise, my father came as soon as he heard. He could not wait another day to see us. When he came into the hotel room, I immediately rushed toward him but then stopped just few inches away from him. I was not sure if I should hug him, but my father could not wait for me to make a move. He hugged me so tight, with tears running down his cheeks, that I started crying too."

"Both my children watched as we were both crying. The three-year-old held my hand and tried to pull me away from Papa. She said, 'Papa, Papa, leave my mom alone.' She looked at me and asked, 'Mommy, is Papa mean to you? Why are you crying?' I had to explain to her that I had tears of joy."

"After we sat down, my father was quiet for few moments, and I wondered what was going on in his mind. He looked happy, and after a quiet moment, he looked at me and called me by my native name, which no one had called me for the past ten years. He said, 'My daughter, I am very sorry. I know I have wronged you and have caused you so much pain and hardship. I want you to forgive me. I know better now not to push you or any of my children away from me ever again.' I was shocked by what he said because I had never heard Father apologize to anyone for anything. Father was always right. His apology sounded sincere and genuine. I accepted his apology, and I also apologized to him for my long silence over the years."

"Well, would wonders never end? I almost fell off the chair when my father told me he was a born-again Christian. I asked with surprise, 'Papa, do you mean you have given your life to God?' I shouted *"alleluia"* at least three times and said to him, 'Papa, only God changes people.' I also told him that God had changed my life through the family that took me in when I went to the city. I said they were my second family now, and I would never forget what they did for me. I let him know also that it takes a good Christian and people with good hearts to truly forgive others."

"Again, my father apologized over and over and said he felt irresponsible that another family had taken on his responsibility of me while he was still alive. I assured Father that I had forgiven him. 'Christians forgive.' Father asked that we move from the hotel to his house, and we did. We spent a happy holiday with him, my step mom, and my siblings; my children enjoyed being around papa. I have had a good relationship with him ever since, and we have visited home with my husband and children many times since then."

"As my father grew further into Christianity, his rigid cultural and traditional beliefs faded; he no longer believed in the tradition that forbade daughters from inheriting their family inheritance. He once said that God created everyone equal and it was against God's will for anyone to discriminate against someone based on gender."

185

"Father is very old now but growing stronger in the Lord. I thank God for everything. I reminded my father over and over to educate his family members and friends on stopping the selfish acts against their female children, because children get hurt by their decisions."

Interview 8

This story is from a young woman who shared the negative effect of polygamy.

"I grew up in a small city in a family of nine. My parents were devoted Christians. Our father was loving and caring; a hard task master but still very involved in our lives. Contrary to the trend back then, he helped with house chores and raising the children. My father took a turn for the worse when I was fifteen years old. We'd just moved back to the capital. While we were adjusting to this new environment, we discovered that our parents' relationship was breaking up. One day, a classmate said that my brother was attending the same school as I was."

"I was shocked since my three older brothers were already working. As we walked along, he pointed to a young man. I'd never seen him, but I took the time to observe him from afar. He looked like my father and my other brothers. In this nightmarish reality, my father had two wives and three other boys. This was a family secret that was well kept, but now it seemed that everyone agreed it was time for us to know each other. My father ensured that all of us were attending the same school and created opportunities to meet informally."

"These were struggling times. We witnessed our mother's misery. Our parents were arguing and raising their voices like never before. Our father would spend days away from home. There was no peace at home. None knew how to deal with this unforeseen crisis. Since most of our siblings were already well established, my two sisters and I were the only kids at home. We sided with Mother and gave Father the cold shoulder. We were ignoring him, giving him attitude to the point of being disrespectful. Our father fell from his pedestal. He became a liar. Everyone was hurting."

"Finally, our older siblings called an emergency meeting. We were told to stay away from our parents' struggles. It was up to our father to deal with his wives. As for us, we had to honor our parents. God didn't say to honor them only if they were good, upright, and loving. Therefore, we each asked for forgiveness. We learned to mend broken relationships. Father lost his godlike aura and his authority. We broke free, but we were still respectful to him as the head of the family."

"In our household, we grew up with cousins; we called them brothers. I would say I'm closer to my cousins than to my other siblings. Yet we have some kind of a relationship. A few years later, during one of our conversations with my father, he told me how much he was worried about his three boys being rejected by their siblings because we have different mothers. In Africa, brothers are each other's keepers. The oldest contributes to the upbringing of his siblings, supporting them financially and emotionally, with their education and other needs."

"Although he later advised my three brothers to never fall for polygamy, he felt the moral obligation to look after his children. Therefore, he divided his time between two wives, two households, and two realities. Father later on told us how grateful he was to Mother for helping him take care of both households. Mother used to manage his monthly pay. She always divided the money for the second household, paid tuition fees for all the kids, and took care of the extended family as well. Mother has a quick temper, but she's very generous. She has a short memory about bad things. Once she gets it off her chest, she moves on."

"A few months before his death, Father terminated his relationship with the second wife. He moved back home, and his other kids came to our home to see him. The second wife had no status in the family, other than as the mother of Father's other three boys. As for our siblings, we've established a relationship; some are closer than the others. The eldest brother, my mother's firstborn, looks after all of us."

"I'm not sure why Father ended up with two wives. In my opinion, it's a shared responsibility of both parents. My mother-in-law doesn't like her much because of her strong personality. They encouraged Father to take another wife to keep her in check. My mother was blamed for birthing mostly girls; so Father has been blessed with three boys from his second wife."

"Through it all, Father taught us by example to take full responsibility for our actions; to learn from our mistakes; to forgive one another; to listen; to be humble; and to learn from other's mistakes as well. Father died a devoted Catholic, at peace with himself and the world."

Children Hurt Too

I n forced marriages and polygamous homes, children are affected negatively. I interviewed few children and adults who grew up in a home where their fathers have multiple wives or their mothers were forced to marry to their fathers. Some of these children find it very difficult to talk about their upbringing. Only very few had positive things to say about their fathers. Some said they lost their relationship with their father when he married another. Some do not know how to describe a good relationship with their father because it was never there.

One young man said, "The war between my mother and her co-wife affected me badly. I grew up being called the 'gold-digger's son.'" He didn't want to go over everything that happened when he was growing up, but he did say that his mother was forced to marry his father at a very young age for two reasons: (1) his grandparents wanted a good and wealthy in-law who would take care of their daughter (his mom); and (2) his father could not have a son from his first wife..

"I was the sixth child and the first son," he said. "After my mother gave birth to me, my father showed some love toward my mother and loved me very much. This resulted in jealousy from my mom's co-wife and my older stepsisters. If my dad bought me something or took me out, it was always trouble. Sometimes to avoid fights in the house, my father did not show his love toward me openly. If I needed something, sometimes he would refused to buy it for me, even if he could afford it, in order to avoid jealousy from the other children and his first wife. If he didn't have the money to buy for everyone else, I would go without it."

"After giving birth to me, my mother could not have another son; she had two girls. My father again went in search of another woman to bear him more male children and brought home a third wife. This woman had two sons and two daughters for him. There were always fights and arguments at home between the three women and my dad, at times over little things. After school, I sometimes went over to my friend's house because I was always afraid that I would walk into an argument or fight at home. Even though my father's third wife had two sons for my father, it did not change the attitude of my older sisters, their mother, and my other siblings toward me; they were all jealous of me. They saw me as the first son who would inherit our father's properties when he died."

"There were a few moments of happiness in the home as well as bad moments. Bad things stay in your memory longer than the good ones, especially when the bad things are more than the good ones. I like my daddy very much, but there were only short memories of the love relationship between us. I remember more of the bad relationship with him. The good times I had with him were when I was just a little boy and before my other brothers came along. My mom went through lot of abuse from him; sometimes they fought because of me, both physically and emotionally. My mom stayed because she had nowhere to go. She always said she needed to stay for our sake. She once said that she endured it because 'what cannot be cured can be endured.'"

"Now that I have grown up and have my freedom, I tried to put the past behind me and move on with my life. In all this, one thing I promised myself was never to expose my children to the same lifestyle or situation. In spite of everything, though, I am grateful to my father that he was able to pay for my education, and I am proud of myself that I was able to focus and got my education.

"My father developed an 'I don't care' attitude toward his wives and children. He became very distant and appeared unhappy and frustrated at times. We saw him struggle financially to keep the family going. Paying school fees for us at times was difficult, but even with his attitude, we knew he somehow cared; he just didn't know how to show it. I think at some point he became disappointed in himself; he did not expect such huge responsibilities and probably did not anticipate the financial burden of raising so many children."

"Things did not go the way he expected. When he was failing to meet the financial demand of his wives and children, he turned his anger on his wives, treating them like outsiders, and he paid little attention to us. Having put himself in a situation where he married three wives and had many children, he'd burned his bridges. It appeared he was no longer comfortable with his decision of marrying three wives, but it was too late for him to change things. Even if Father had let go of two or all three wives, it would not have helped solve his financial problems because he would still have had to care for all the children on his own, financially and morally, which was not possible. It appeared he chewed what he could not swallow. As they say, 'Be careful what you wish for.'"

"Father denied us love and affection, but in spite of everything, we respected and listened to him. If we hadn't, we would have lost our chances of getting an education, and we all wanted to be educated. We did not like the situation we grew up in and knew that if we were not educated, we would not be able to make a difference in our children's lives. Plus, we were at the mercy of our father."

"Father's distance from us bothered us a lot, but we could not change his attitude. We only saw examples of how responsible and respectful fathers treated their children by watching other fathers. I watched my friends do things and have fun with their fathers, but I couldn't do the same with my father."

"Looking back, there were lots of awkward, tense moments in the house. I wish I could have changed certain things but it was impossible. Children have no say in the decisions their parents make in their lives."

As I've mentioned, in some cultures, a father's relationship with his sons are not same as the relationship with his daughters; this includes communication. The distance between father and son and father and daughter is more obvious in the villages than in the cities. It may be because most fathers in the cities are educated and civilized. Some fathers are closed-minded to their daughters and have little communication with them. Their daughters are afraid to talk to them or approach them about their personal problems; they are afraid of being ignored or yelled at if they say the wrong things. They only go to their mothers for certain things because mothers listen.

In some cases, daughters are only able to talk openly with their fathers after they grow up and sometimes after they leave home. The consequences for fathers who are distant from their children are that they do not know their children very well, especially their daughters, and their children do not know them well either. The distance between husbands and wives in some cultures is even greater. It is almost like husbands neglect their wives. This leads to many divorces, and when this happens, the children suffer even more.

Children are affected differently by their parents' divorce. Their ages, parental support, family support, and society support at the time of the divorce determines how well they cope. Children are often left neglected in the process, especially in a culture where only a man can decide when to divorce his wife. Some children are emotionally damaged because they do not have the maturity to deal with what happened in their lives and have no power to change things.

In some cases, children may blame themselves for the divorce. They may feel they caused it or that they did something or said something to make their parents mad. Divorce is hurtful to children, regardless of which parent is at fault. It is very important to think about the effects that divorce has on children when taking such action. As parents, you need to consider the emotional damage that divorce may have on your child.

If it is possible to save your marriage and resolve your issues, please do so for the sake of your children. If you divorced one wife or husband and marry another, remember that the second marriage may not be perfect. Consider trying everything possible to save your marriage, including professional or traditional counseling, as this benefits everyone involved.

If you try everything to save your marriage and fail, you can now prepare your children to accept the circumstances. Do not blame one another or point fingers at each other before your children, especially if they are too young to understand. Even if one of you did not agree to the divorce, accept it, and try to move on, instead of hoping or preparing your children for a dream that may never come true. Parents with older children find it easier to adjust and move on than the ones with young children. For this reason, extra help is needed for the young children to be able to cope. Even years after the divorce, your children may believe that someday, somehow, the two of you will get back together, and you will be one happy family again; this is what most children hope and dream. If this does not happen, they can turn their hopes into anger, and depression may set in. This may also lead them to bad behavior.

In societies where sole custody of children is granted to the father, some fathers marry another wife just after the divorce to replace their divorced wife. If you remarry, especially soon after your divorces, children may turn their anger on their stepmothers for taking their mother's place. They may rebel and be disrespectful to their stepmothers, and sometimes they may be angry at their father for letting their mother go. This can result in building a wall between them and their stepmother, ending a good relationship with their stepmothers before it even starts. It may also lead to unhealthy stepmother and stepchildren relationships. If your children's behavior changes after your divorce, which is most likely, seek counseling for them and for the whole family.

Every child's dream is to live with Mom and Dad and have a relationship with both of them. In my day, marriages did not fall apart as quickly as they do today because men and women compromised and remained married for a very long time; in most cases, until death do them part.

Divorce is difficult for children because the only parents and lifestyle they know is shifted away, through no fault of their own. As children, we believe that our parents will be together forever. No child at a young age ever anticipates divorce or separation of their parents, and when this happens, they become angry. No matter how parents try to explain or sugar-coat divorce to children, they do not accept it easily; all that matters to them is that their lives will be with only mother or only father taking care of them, which takes away the happy family.

As parents, look for signs and help your children as soon as possible. Groups of people, organizations, and books can help children cope with grief. My first book, *The Agony of a Mother*, helps to understand children's grief, the signs to look for in children, and how to best help children cope with grief. Education, counseling, advocate groups, and outreach have helped many children to recover quickly from depression cause by divorce and other tragedies in the family.

The Bible says that the only grounds for divorce are fornication or sex outside of marriage, but there are other reasons that may lead to divorce. For example, a woman is forced to marry a man she does not love and is mistreated by her husband. She may want to find a way out of the marriage. Holding a wife hostage may be another reason for a woman to get out of the situation. Neglect or wife abuse (physical and emotional) may also lead to divorce, and starving a wife may be another reason for divorce. Inresposibilities of husband or wife or both may be another reason for divorce.

If marriage becomes unbearable for the above reasons and divorce is an option. You can ask for divorce in a way that your children do not suffer too much. Again, remember that it is not your children's choice to divorce. Make sure you prepare your children for the worst, and arrange counseling and other resources for them before their negative behavior starts.

Remaining in the marriage is best for children and the whole family if the marriage is healthy. But it is not always possible for people to save their marriages. Many women who experienced bad relationships and unhealthy marriages that eventually led to divorce have said they are better off without a husband than staying in an unhealthy marriage. "It is better to eat crumbs in a peaceful environment than to have a banquet in a big house full of trouble." In spite of the above, some women stay because they have nowhere to go. Whether there are children in your marriage or not, when your marriage is life-threatening for you and unsafe for your children, you will have to consider safety first, and move you and children out of the environment. Women that choose to stay; no matter what, may get killed in the process, when trying to fix the unfixable and change the unchangeable.

Why Abused Wives Stay in a Marriage

Why do women stay in an abusive and unhealthy relationship? Sometimes they stay because they have no choice. They are controlled by their husbands or partners and cannot decide what is best for them and their children. Remember that a controlled mind makes no decision of its own.

One of the ladies I interviewed said, "It is very hard to stay in an abusive relationship or marriage, and it is hard to get out once you are in. The husbands take their wives' freedom and power away from them, reduce their self-esteem, and make them feel worthless. They don't feel they can make it on their own. The husband criticizes everything his wife does or says, puts her down, takes credit for her effort, and make her feel less important at any chance he gets, even in public. You would only understand this if you are in the situation."

Sometimes if these women try to do something about their situation or just try to get their points across to their husbands, they are shut down and reminded over and over that they are just women and have no rights. Fortunately, some women are becoming educated and more aware of their abusive situations; recognizing the situation is a step forward to correcting the wrongs.

The biggest problem with some abused women is that they do not recognize abuse or control and often take their husband's abusive behavior as the norm. They are also stuck because their environment is "polluted with control." They accept it and feel somewhat comfortable. Many stay for fear of losing their children; they fear that their husbands will take their children away from them if they leave or talk back.

As mentioned, in most African cultures, fathers are given sole custody of their children after divorce, regardless of his ability to provide good care. If he is unable to take care of his children, he can get help from his parents or other relatives. If he has another wife in the home, the wife would take on the responsibilities of the children. If there is a grown-up daughter among the children, the daughter would assume the role of the mother, caring for her siblings, cooking, cleaning, and doing other housework.

Men have the right in some cultures to deprive the children of seeing their mother at any time, even if the children want to see their mothers. If the children disobey their father, he can cut them off financially and, in some cases, disown them. It is sad, but this is an everyday practice that is part of life in some Africa cultures.

Woman may feel trapped in an unhealthy or toxic marriage. Some women hope to change their husbands' controlling behavior, but they fail to realize that to change someone else's behavior is difficult. You can only change yourself. "You can lead a horse to the river, but you can't make him drink." Many stay because they have no education, no money, no job, and no family support; some also stay because they are afraid of the unknown. As they say, "The devil you know is better than the one you don't know."

Few men stay in unhealthy relationships as well because they find it difficult to ask for divorce if theirs was an arranged or forced marriage. They do not want to offend the parents who arranged the marriage and forced the wives on them. Some men are under the control of their parents as well. Instead of letting go of the marriage, they live in a hateful and unhealthy marriage and behave strangely. Most of these affected men are from wealthy parents; they depend on their parents financially. Even if some of these men have jobs, they may be working for their fathers or running their fathers' businesses and do not want to lose their source of income. For some of them, the only work they've ever done is with their fathers. They fear they won't find employment anywhere else if their father terminates their employment or forbids them from running the family business. Some men stay in a marriage to protect their family honor.

Some men live as strangers or roommates with their wives; some are only close to their wives intimately once in a while, when they want to make love to her for the sake of pleasing themselves sexually or having children. Some resent that the wife is in the house but can't ask her to leave for fear of what the parents and society will say or think. He does not show any interest in what the wife does; his wife may be a beautiful woman and of the best behavior, but because there is no love between them, he does not see the beauty in her. He tries to keep her in the house just to please his parents and lives in a marriage that was not meant to be. He fails to realize how much he is displeasing himself by pleasing his parent. Those men who depend on their parents, financially or otherwise, may be afraid that they will lose financial support if they ask their wives to leave. Or he may be cut off from his family inheritance that awaits him when his father dies. Some rich men force their sons and daughters to marry a person from a rich family for business and financial gains. Sometimes if their son refuses the marriage, their ties to the business may also fail; for that reason they do everything to keep the marriage together, even if it is unhealthy.

Women (and a few men) in forced marriages gave the following reasons for staying with their spouse:

- Nowhere to go
- No family support
- No financial support
- Afraid her husband will kill her if she leaves
- Believes she can change his behavior
- Believes he will stop beating her
- Thinks violence is normal in a marriage
- Feels jealousy is a sign of love
- Thinks if she has children for him, he will change his attitude
- Blames herself for being hit; feels she must have provoked it

- Low self-esteem
- Afraid to be alone
- Feelings of shame and guilt
- Fear of letting her children down
- Cultural and religious reasons
- Thinks it is shameful to divorce
- Not aware of available resources
- Losing control of herself
- Believes the situation will change
- Thinks she can never make it on her own
- Afraid society will condemn her if she leaves.
- Thinks sexual abuse is part of lovemaking
- Thinks if he does not love her now, he will later
- Think he will send her back to her parents if she disobeys him
- Her parents told her never to leave him or come back home to them
- To support her children
- Afraid her husband may deny her financial support
- To give stable home for her children
- She does not want to remove her children from their stable environment
- To watch her children grow
- To prevent other women from raising her children
- She does not want to be seen as a failure
- For cultural practices
- She does not have a job and money to care for her children

Most of these women are afraid of what their husbands would do to them if they leave. Many girls and women have been killed by their husbands or husband's family for trying to escape. Nothing happens to the men, because society allows honor-killing. Other crimes have also been committed in the name of forced marriages. This is still happening in most African countries, as well as in Afghanistan and parts of India. There is no love in forced marriages; it is plastered with sorrow and stress.

Women who stay in such marriages keep the stress, pain, and sorrow to themselves. In some cultures, you are not allowed to express feelings of marital pain openly. No one cares about women's complains or takes reports of their marital abuse seriously.

Forced Marriages, Stress, and Depression.

Most people believe that stress is only brought about by such things as death, divorce, loss of job, or sickness. Under some circumstances, the body reacts negatively to certain events. People sometimes receive help, but in the case of marital stress, especially in an uncivilized world, marital depression, which is almost as painful or disturbing as death or illness, is not taken seriously. Women are not expected to talk about it, so they suffer in silence because they have nowhere to turn. Most women who are forced to marry suffer loss of freedom and recognition when their fathers force them from the only family they know to a total stranger in the name of marriage.

In forced marriages, most women are denied every right, freedom, and independence and are expected to do what their husbands tell them. Most young women struggle with the strict rules and control and the overwhelming responsibilities their husbands and in-laws place on them. Some have to fight endlessly for their rights, but unfortunately, only few succeed in gaining independence. Others remain in bondage and under the dictatorship of their husbands. These girls face hardships because of their husbands, but they also struggle with their in-laws.

Interview 9

This last interview, from a young lady from Nigeria, is a bit different in the sense that her mother, who was supposed to protect her, worked with her husband behind the daughter's back to plan her marriage. Even worse, she used a juju ritual to ensure that her daughter got married to the man she chose for her. It is most common in this culture that fathers dictate to whom their daughters get married. In this case, her mother was the one behind every arrangement.

"My story of growing up in a polygamous home is of nostalgia and very intriguing, not at the time but in retrospect. I grew up in Benin City, Nigeria, in West Africa. My household of a patriarchal rule is culturally where the man suppresses the women and rules over everyone else in the home. My dad was just starting his transportation business when he met my mother, who at that time was leaving a very bad marriage that resulted in a son. My dad was also just ending a relationship that produced two children. Both of them were in need of each other. They got married under the customs and tradition of my people (Edo)."

"My mother inherited a huge cocoa farm from her late father, which was then sold to some cocoa importers, and my mother got a significant amount of money from the transaction. Marital relationships were patriarchal in nature so my mother gave all her earnings to my dad, which he invested in his business and purchased more vehicles."

"Problems began to brew in our home when my aunties realized that my mother had an Itsekiri lineage (another tribe in Edo state of Nigeria). The Edo people believe that Itsekiri women will kill their husbands to inherit their wealth. However, they forgot how my dad acquired his blossoming wealth. So with my paternal grandmother and my aunties constantly causing problems in our home, my dad was pressured to get married to another woman. I remember vividly the day the woman was brought to our home. She came in wearing a brown dress, holding a brown bag, which was the only property that she owned. She was a maid to a woman who lived just few houses from our home. She was from a very poor home, uneducated, and very timid. My mother accepted this woman and cleaned her up so that she was socially acceptable."

"My dad was beginning to be very successful; his business was booming, and he began to participate in political activities and was a socialite. Typically for his status at that time, he became promiscuous and even brought another woman home. At the end of the day, my dad was officially married to three women and had numerous concubines, and some of them had children for him."

"Polygamous living has its own dynamic. My dad was able to manage the home as best as he could. I will say that Dad provided for everyone in the family, including extended family members. The interesting thing that I remember is that Dad always had a favorite wife; it was the second wife, and then some other women in between, and then the third wife."

"The third wife came in because my father's family members were complaining that my mother and the second wife were not educated, so they brought a young woman who was the same age as my eldest sister and had a standard four education, which is equivalent to the present-day grade ten education. Interestingly, she was not able to read or write, to everyone's amazement. My dad had a weekly schedule for the three wives. The wife that was cooking for the two weeks would be the wife sleeping with my dad. It seemed to work well for the wives, but occasionally the third wife would steal some days of the second wife, which always broke out in a fight. There was so much jealousy, animosity, hatred, and ongoing competition in the house, especially between the second and the third wife and among their children. My mother was respected by all, but conflicts arose on occasion with the other wives."

"As we all grew up, the competition became worse, and the use of spiritual means came into play. Eventually, I lost one of my brothers. There are so many disadvantages to having multiple wives, as there is bound to be inequality that will lead to hatred, animosity, and negativity in the home, which is carried into adulthood for the children born into such homes."

"The disadvantages of polygamy greatly outweigh the advantages, if there are any. The history of polygamy is as old as creation, even in the days of Old Testament Bible. Different cultures practice polygamy for different reason—beliefs, culture, and traditions. At a time in my Edo culture, it was and still is acceptable for a man to marry many women, and all the wives live under one roof, which creates strange dynamics."

"My second story of being forced into a marriage was chosen by my mother. When I was in the university, I had a boyfriend who was in medical school. I loved him so much, and his parents loved me so much that when I visited his parents, I would sit on his father's lap. We were friends throughout university and after graduation; he went for his horsemanship youth corps services and got a job at the state hospital, while I got a job in a dental clinic in my state. His parents contacted my parents to begin the preparation for marriage. My mother was totally against this union because the man was from another tribe. She did everything within her power to separate us and even used diabolical means."

"At about the same time, I met my ex-husband, who was very arrogant, rude, and a typically dominant man. I did not like him a bit because while growing up, I witnessed my dad's behavior toward my mother, and I swore that I would not get married to a man from my tribe. Anyway, the diabolical means worked, because all of a sudden, I began to forget about my boyfriend, and within a short period, my mother and my ex-husband started to plan my wedding, to the extent that my mother purchased the wedding ring."

"A very strange event occurred; my ex-husband coerced me and took me to two spiritualists, and when I got home, I told my mother, and she said that it was okay. Apparently, my mother was in support of the visit. I later learned that my ex-husband wanted to lock me into the marriage for fear that I would leave him; he was twelve years older than me. Thank God for his saving grace. We got married, and I moved with him to a different state."

"During the wedding preparation, it looked like I was in a kind of trance. That lasted until he beat me up two weeks after the wedding. He hit me so hard that I passed out, and my neighbors took me to the hospital. When I woke up, I could not believe that I was married. Apparently, the spiritualist told him that in order to maintain the black magic, he should not beat me. Anyway, that was the beginning of my sorrow; the beating became very constant, and every argument resulted in a slap across the face or the tearing of my clothes, even in the public places. He dislocated my shoulder; broke my neck, and presently, I have 85 percent hearing loss in my left ear. I was married to him for fourteen years of immense physical, sexual, emotional, spiritual, and financial abuse. He would refer to me as "just a woman" in very derogatory ways. I sought help from my mother and pastors in the church; all I got was "be submissive and be patient." It was such a terrible, dark time in my life. I hated him so much that I had to be drunk to have any intimate time with him; I had to be disconnected from my body and mind. Thank God for immigrating to Canada. That was when I got my freedom from the nightmare."

"Upon coming to Canada, the abuse continued. We went for professional counseling and counseling in the church. Both counselors advised me to file for divorce. I was afraid to file for divorce because I did not want the stigma attached to a divorced woman, especially in the context of my cultural and religious beliefs. I am a born-again Christian. So I continued in the relationship. He refused to work, so I was responsible for the running of the home, and the abuse intensified until he started cheating on me with my very good friend."

"They both, as they confessed, were trying to get "rid" of me. They both decided to send my name to witch doctors in Nigeria. They said that they sent my name to three witch doctors, and the last one warned them to leave me alone, that each time he tried to summon my spirit and hurt me, a wall of fire would surround me. It was at this time my friend came over to my home and said that she had to confess."

"My ex-husband and my friend confessed to all their evil deeds; she had even attempted to poison my food, but for some reason, I did not eat the food. Coincidentally, my mother was visiting at the time, so she had the opportunity to confess to how my ex-husband tied me into the marriage. This was when I decided to leave the marriage, which was a very difficult, nasty breakup."

"You may wonder and ask questions about forgiveness. I forgive my mother and ex-husband. In retrospect, my mother thought that she was doing me a favor by forcing me to get married to a man from my tribe. My ex-husband has undiagnosed mental issues, and I feel so sorry for him. Thank God Almighty that I got married again to a wonderful man who loves and respects me. Thank God for my children, for they have wiped away tears from my eyes. Thanks to the author for providing me such an opportunity to tell my story. I hope it will serve as a deterrent to parents so they will not make such mistakes."

Luckily, this young lady was able to break free from her husband's brutality and her mother's marital control over many years. Unfortunately, many girls are not so lucky; some remain in such situations forever, and many die before they can escape. Some have fought and died in the process of freeing themselves.

CHAPTER
30

Struggle with In-Laws

In most African countries and some Nigerian traditions and cultures, girls are not only forced to marry strangers, but they also are forced to live with their in-laws and their husband's extended family members for observation, for as long as the in-laws think is needed to approve of her marriage to their son and approve of her staying with her husband. It may take weeks, months, or longer, and if her husband resides with them permanently, this also becomes her permanent residence. It is cultural believe that when you are married to a man, you are married to the entire family. They expect her, from that time on, to assume all the responsibilities of what they believed to be housewife duties; to cook and do all the duties and housework.

As it is mostly the practice in Africa cultures, newlyweds are not given privacy; there is hardly any private moment with her and her husband, as they are always surrounded with visitors, both close family and extended family members; all the time. The new wife is expected to cook for these visitors.

If a new wife is unlucky, and some of the husband's close family members, especially her mother in-law, finds fault in her and considers her not to be good enough for her son, that may be the end of the marriage that never began. Many marriages have fallen apart or ended before they even started, based on her in-law's assumption of her. In most cases, her husband has no say in his marriage; he goes along with his family's decision, as he too believes that "mother knows best." (This saying may be true in other cases but should not apply to marriages.)

The wife experiences fights and arguments with her in-laws most times, over little things such as how well she performed house chores, and how well she relates to others in the family. She is expected to respect all members of her husband's family, even if they do not respect her. She may be abused during this time of observation. She does not report the abuse for the fear of being called a bad wife; she keeps the abuse to herself. In societies where in-laws control their sons and daughters-in-law, the woman in this situation is always afraid to report her in-laws to her husband, afraid of what the consequences would be if she did.

Whatever abuse and insults she receives from her in-laws, she keeps to herself. She believes it is better not to report her concerns to her husband than to report and be ignored. She keeps her feelings and issues to herself. She also may fear that her husband will support his family and tell her to accept things as they are. He believes that his family is teaching her how to be a good wife. She stands alone, without her husband's support.

In some cultures, as soon as a woman get married, her husband's and her in-laws' responsibilities become hers, but hers don't matter to them. She is expected to assist her husband in caring for her husband's family, especially her husband's younger siblings, if any. If she and her husband live in the family home with his parents, her mother-in-law would become her big baby. She is expected to cook, clean, wash her clothes, and run errands for her. Even if her mother-in-law has other grown children residing at home, she expects her daughter-in-law to do everything. Some mothers-in-law treat their daughters-in-law like their servants.

She is expected to serve them as well as her husband. If she fails to obey their orders, she is considered a bad wife, and as a result, they may ask her husband to send her back to her parents. In this culture, it is considered shameful for a woman to marry and be sent back to her parents because she is unable to perform her duties as a wife. To avoid being sent back, she stays in the abusive situation.

In a civilized world, in-laws are never the responsibility of the wives. Children gain their independence way before they get married, and once they are married, they both leave their fathers and mothers and start their lives together and become one flesh. This is according to the Bible (Ephesians 5:31). Also in civilized countries, parents back out once their children are married, and they avoid invading their privacy.

In most African cultures, parents do not allow their sons to grow up; they do not teach them independence at a young age, and they never want them to leave home, especially their first son. In some cases when a father is building a house, he includes an apartment for his first son in the compound, as he expects him to stay there for the rest of his life, even after he is married. The wife is expected to move in with him in the family house. This mostly leads to marriage disaster. Living with your husband in a family house with his family just after you get married can be a blessing or disaster in your marriage; they can be the light or darkness in your marriage. If they don't like you, they can influence your husband's behavior negatively. Some men act on the advice and complaints they get from their parents and siblings and feel that their families are more important than their wives. They may believe that "blood is thicker than water."

Many men refer to their parents, siblings, and other extended family members as their family but to the wife as just a woman and his children as just children. He considers his duties to his "family" to be more important than to his wife and children. There have been many cases where a husband divorces his wife because she does not respect his mother, or she talks back to his mother. It does not matter whether his mother deserves the respect or whether his mother respects his wife. To him, it is one-way traffic. Some of these men marry more than once; sometimes both lead to divorce due to his mother's or other family members' involvement in his marriages. Some realize very late that their lives have been ruined by their family's misjudgment of their wives, but by then, it is too late to change things.

Parents may encourage their son's wife to move into the family home because they are afraid that if they distance themselves from their son, especially their first son, he may abandon them in their old age. They believe that out of sight is out of mind.

Many parents hold tight to their first son, much as they hold on to their precious and personal properties. These parents fear that their daughters-in-law will take their sons away from them when he gets married. Some of the decisions these parents make are based on fear of the unknown, which may explain why they want their children to remain with them even after they get married, so they can monitor the son and the wife and have control over both. These parents many force a wife on their sons; in most cases, they look for a woman they can control. The reason they do this is because they want to maintain the same bond and control over their son, even after he is married. In this culture, the control parents have over their children never fades but gets stronger as they age.

In some cultures, it is only recently that a first son is allowed to have a say on a woman his parents choose for him. It is only recently that their first son is allowed to marry someone from another culture. They have a special control over their first son, as it is culturally believed that the first son is a wise son. Even within the family, the control they have over their first sons is not the same as other sons or other children. It is also only recently in some parts of Africa that fathers willingly agree and allow their first sons to travel far away from home or to other countries. They see this as a final separation from their sons.

It formerly was forbidden for their sons to marry a foreigner; especially their first son. Marrying a woman from a different culture was enough reason (and still is in some cultures) for parents to disown their son. It was like the reaction some white people had over their sons or daughters marrying blacks, even now in some communities.

They regard this as losing their culture altogether. There have been cases where their first sons traveled out of their countries and married women different from those in their own culture. When this happens, the parents do not take it kindly. In some cases, they put an end to their children's marriage and also fail to recognize children born as a result of these marriages. They also fail to accept the first male child from "intercultural marriages" and deny him the inheritance that may be due to the first child. Some put pressure on their sons until they marry a second wife, or divorce the foreigner and marry from their own culture.

When their son marries, the wife is sometimes not allowed to work outside the home, and if she does, she is expected to hand over her paycheck to her husband. Men in this culture treat their wives as paychecks, and his family treats her as just a wife. A wife should not have anything of her own, only what she is given by her husband. She may be working and earning more money and contributing more to the family, both financially and morally, to support her family, but her contribution does not count. All credit goes to her husband. Everything a woman owns, in most Africa cultures, belongs to her husband. Her name is forbidden to appear on anything her husband owns, including his house or houses, landed properties, and his money. Some educated immigrant men's behavior in this culture is not far from their fathers' behavior.

I have seen many young educated men here in Canada who have emigrated from Africa whose behavior is worse than that of their fathers back home. Some of these men treat their wives just as their fathers treated their mothers. Some are refusing to take life insurance or invest in housing properties here. They see anything owned or jointly owned that would involve their wives' names as losing their properties to their wives. They do not want their life insurance to name their wives as beneficiaries. After their divorce from their wives, some are refusing to work or take reasonable employment and quit their good-paying jobs to avoid paying child support, as they see supporting their children financially as also supporting their wives financially. They watch from afar how their ex-wives struggle to bring up their children and sometimes with government assistant. Some take insurance and make their relatives the beneficiaries; others go home to their countries and invest in properties without including their wives' names, and sometimes the wives are not even aware. With some, their children never know the whereabouts of their properties. When the father dies, his family members take over his properties and money. Even after a man's death, his wife and children are treated as outsiders.

A woman in some cultured is enslaved for life, not only by her husband but also by her in-laws. Some sisters-in-law are as powerful as the mother. Stepping into her mother's place, she takes over the control of her brother's wife and feels it's her duty to teach her sister in-law how she should care for her brother and how to be a good housewife. She believes this is what her mother would have done. If her sister-in-law refuses to follow her instructions, she may see this as disobedient and may do anything in her power to end her marriage to her brother. In these cultures, some sons have the same trust in their big sisters as they have in their mothers.

Women have to be resentful and fight back to gain independence from their husbands and in-laws; otherwise, they will turn her into a subdued wife. A woman who is married to a man from family that look to their sons (especially their first sons) for everything has to fight extra hard to break free. Her in-laws may see her as coming between them and their son. Some parents who have nothing to rely on in their old age and who are depending on their sons for everything believe that their sons are their "pension." They do not want any woman to take away their future benefits. These parents have no boundaries; they control their sons from the time they are young and continue even after marriage. Some use spiritual power to control their sons. Some men in these cultures allow their mothers to control their wives as well.

In most African traditions, some men complain about their wives to their mothers and family members for any little problem. They expect their family to pass judgment on their wives. If their mother decides that she is not a good wife, based on the complaint from the son, she may ask the son to divorce her, and some sons would do just that. If he refuses to divorce her, his parents and extended family members regard this as disobedience and may cut the bond between him and the family; or worse, cut him out of their will, especially if he is from a rich family. Some sons that broke away from their parents' control face criticism from not only their parents but his extended family members. His parents sometimes turn their anger on his wife and think that he is under her control. In a culture that believes in witchcraft, in-laws may accuse their daughter-in-law of bewitching their son. Married men in some cultures are never wrong. If anything happens to him, they blame it on his wife.

Failures in some marriages are as a result of men reporting their wives to their family and not handling their marital problem on their own. By so doing, they expose their marriage to failure. In-laws may be welcoming and supportive of their daughter-in-laws; there are many caring, loving, and God-fearing in-laws who accept their daughter-in-laws and open their hearts. They treat their daughters-in-laws as their own and as part of their family. They can be a good support to their sons and daughters-in-laws, morally and financially. In times of trouble, they can also help them settle their problems, and in time of financial need, they can also help them out.

Some in-laws act selfishly due to poverty. If their son/brother has been financially responsible for them before his marriage, they may take this as a loss of income, as they believe that the money will now be spent on his wife instead of them. In some cultures in Africa, children become responsible for their parents, financially and morally, as soon as they finish school and get a job, especially the first sons and occasionally daughters. The son's contribution to his parents and close family members would depend on how much he makes.

If they totally or partially depend on their son's income for their survival, some in-laws may become very upset at the changes their son's or brother's marriage may bring to them, even if they support his marriage at first. They may also see this as loss of time spent with him, as they believe his focus and attention will be more on his wife. These in-laws may try to criticize the wife for everything she does. If the wife is from a poor family and uneducated, this may even open more doors for criticizing her.

With most girls forced to marry, even those who are educated, are always under the watchful eyes of their husbands' families. The family is always afraid the new wife will run away. Employment outside of the home or keeping her own bank account is not allowed in some cases, as this may further cause suspicion and problems between her husband and his family.

Also, it is their belief that she is supposed to be home at all times to serve them; this is expected of a "proper housewife."

Watch for the following signs in a controlling relationship with in-laws:

- They blame you for their son's behavior
- They watch your every move
- They condemn your actions
- They accuse you of taking their son away from them
- They tell you that you are worthless
- They say negative things to your husband about you
- Nothing you do is good enough for them
- They put you down any chance they get
- They treat you like a servant
- They want their son to ask their permission before he does anything for you
- They accuse you of coming between them and their son
- They blame you if their son no longer spends the same amount of money and time with them as he did before he married you.
- They want to have their son to themselves
- They behave unkindly and unfriendly toward you
- They disrespect you, even if you respect them
- They don't regard you as part of the family
- They physically and emotionally abuse you
- They blame you for their son's failure in life

Be aware of these signs and stop these actions as early as you can. In most cases, in-laws' control never stops unless you fight back; some don't stop until they drive the wife away. Try to correct the wrongs before it is too late. If you must remove a tree from the garden, it is easier removed before the roots grow deeper into the ground.

I am not saying that women should be rude or fight with their in-laws without reason. A wife must be humble and respectful to her husband and her in-laws. On the other hand, her husband and his family members must also be respectful to her. Respect is mutual; it should be earned and not forced. You get back what you put out, so you will get back respect when you respect others. It is your right as a woman not to take abuse from your husband and in-laws, so exercise your right.

A woman who takes abuse from her husband and in-laws and watches her daughter being abuse by her husband and does nothing takes abuse as the norm. She exercises the same control and abuse of her daughter-in-law and expects the daughter-in-law to also take her abusive behavior as normal and respect her. She finds it very hard to respect her daughter-in-law and thinks respect should be a one-way street.

If you want to see your daughter happy in her husband's house, free from her husband's and in-laws' control and abuse, you must treat your daughters and daughter-in-laws with respect first. If you disrespect your daughter, others may take advantage of her wherever she goes. Be a good role model in your children's lives, and they will grow up with your respect.

The majority of girls forced to marry are regarded as property and sexual objects by their husbands and his family members treat her as servant. They are forced to behave in a way that pleases their husbands and are placed where their husbands want them to be. In some cultures, some forced girls are enslaved for life, even after the death of their husbands. When a man dies, a member of his family (his brother or uncle) can take the husband's place. He marries her and assumes responsibility as her husband, as well as taking responsibility of her children. He can also inherit her husband's properties, especially where there is no male child or if the male child is not of an age to assume responsibility for himself and others.

Girls forced to marry are primarily victims of violence, and most end up in polygamous marriages. Women in polygamous marriages experience more abuse than those in monogamous marriages and are forced, in most cases, to stay home as full-time housewives. Full-time housewives experience a higher incidence of abuse than married women who are employed outside the home, just as educated women suffer less abuse than illiterates at the hand of their husbands. Tradition, in some cases, encourages some of these abusive behaviors toward girls and women in many societies in Africa.

CHAPTER 31

Harmful Tradition/Forced Marriage

The high incidence of abuse against girls and women in most African countries is as a result of the traditional system. It does apply to boys sometimes, but it affects more girls than boys. This is a dangerous traditional practice that must be stopped.

The husband in most cases has cut off the wife from her family members, friends, and the outside world. He does not allow her to work, go to school, or socialize with others. If he lives outside of his country with his wife, he may allow her to work for financial help. Men like these treat their wives as a paycheck. They allow their wives to work but do not allow them to spend any of the money they earn on themselves. These wives are not allowed to have their own accounts; the husband dictates how the money is spent.

He demands to know her every move; he does not allow her to go anywhere without him or without his permission. He asks her to dress to his taste and reduces her to the point of feeling worthless in order to gain total control of her.

I worked with a lady many years ago. I thought her marriage was one of the best. To an outsider, it seemed like everything was great. Her husband used to drop her at work daily and pick her up as soon as she finished work. She kept to herself, even at work, and did not say much about her marriage or family; no one knew there was anything wrong with her marriage. Suddenly, her marriage fell apart after about ten years. She later told us that her husband was using her as a paycheck; she was allowed to work but not allowed to have her own account. Her husband was only dropping her off and picking her up because he believed that if she was left on her own, she would go somewhere else before or after work. She was not allowed to go out nor have friends over to her house.

I am not sure how she broke out of his control. After that, she took some time off work but did not return. Some said she moved away from her husband to a different city. Other men use this type of control on their wives as well. They make them feel lonely and worthless in order to gain total control. A lonely wife is a fearful wife. She would be afraid to leave her husband as she might think she is not good enough and that no other man would want her. This act is not peculiar to men with wives in forced marriages; this also happens in other marriages and relationships. Controlling men have no boundaries.

A controlling man watches his wife's every move. He takes charge of the family and makes decisions for her and the family. He condemns other women who are in control and makes her feel that her situation is better than theirs. He tells her what to wear, what to do, when to do it, and how to do it. He inspects everything she does, he questions every move she makes, and he judges her for every mistake she makes. He expects her to obey his commands without question. He wants her to depend on him for everything. He makes her believe that emotional and physical abuse is normal in a marriage and wants her to accept it.

If he abuses her emotionally, without physical abuse, he wants her to believe that it is not abuse because there are no physical scars. He stops her from talking to anyone about his abusive behavior and threatens to divorce her if she does. Physical abuse is the most noticeable form of abuse because there are scars, but emotional abuse is equally damaging. Both types of abuse are involved in forced marriages.

An abusive man blames his wife for his behavior. He makes her believe that it is her fault that he abuses her, and he does not accept responsibility for his actions. He makes her believe that he cannot change his attitude because this is who he is. Such behavior and abuse may have been learned from his father, and he feels it is the right way to be in control of his wife.

These men want their wives to believe that they were born with such behavior, and control is part of their upbringing. Fathers and husbands, however, can control their behavior. Behavior is learned, not inborn. If fathers can control their behavior outside the homes and do not abuse, insult, or threaten people outside the home, then it is obvious that they can control their behavior at home with their loved ones as well, if they choose to.

A caring and loving father does not save his frustration or anger for his loved ones over issues that happened outside of his home, in public. He deals with it publicly and talks about it maturely. A father who chooses when and how to abuse his loved ones and can act normally in public, as if he has the best behavior, and only loses his temper on his wife or children at home is nothing but a controlling father and husband. There are cases where women call the police on their husbands during a fight or physical abuse. When the police arrive, their husbands immediately act their best and sometimes smile and change their tone of voice to make it look like the argument was not serious and should not be a concern to the police. When they get to work immediately after a fight with their wives, they act their best and perform their daily tasks efficiently, as if nothing has happened at home.

Some change their behavior toward their wives and children for few days following the police call, giving them the impression that they have changed and giving the family hope for the best. This is because they do not want the police to be called again or do not want to go to jail in a country where the law applies. If these fathers can switch their moods when they want to, they can also be of good behavior if they want. Don't be fooled when a man tells you that he is behaving the way he does because of his upbringing and his culture and that he cannot change. This may be true to some extent but upbringing is not totally responsible for his behavior, and it can be changed.

Once again, women have to remember that these behaviors with men are not inborn. They are learned and seen; therefore, it can also be unlearned, and changes can be made. The fact is that control and abuse is a choice.

If these men went to school, they may have learned a new trade or languages, and sometimes they are very good at learning those trades. They can also learn good manners as well, if they didn't learn from their parents growing up.

The example of learned behavior in marriage is this: When some African men go to America, Canada, the UK, or other places where the law of marriage protects women and prosecutes men who abuse their wives; these men adjust and abide by the rules of the country, especially when they are married to women from a different culture. If these men can easily adjust and obey the law and rules of their new country and control their tempers, they can easily treat their wives and children better if they want to. As I earlier stated, violence is a selfish act of control. Girls forced to marry are controlled by their husbands, and they also face serious other problems, especially in the early marriages. Some of these problems include:

- Divorce
- Transmitted diseases
- Premature death
- Abuse
- Health problems
- Control
- Isolation
- Jealousy and abandonment
- Low self-esteem
- Physical and emotional abuse

An abusive husband can be an abusive father. Some abusive and controlling husbands transfer their attitude to their children, especially their male children. An abusive father finds a way to blame his children or wife for his behavior and holds them responsible for provoking him. Such fathers and husbands act cowardly. If he has a bad day at work or with his friends, he brings his anger home and releases it on his wife or children. Some come home after losing money to gambling and put their anger on their children and wives. This behavior is a selfish act.

Some fathers that forced their underage children into marriage say it is an act of love, protection, and discipline. They say they love their daughters and want them to have good husbands and good homes. There is nothing good about a home without love. These fathers have to know the difference between discipline, protection, love, and abuse. There is a big difference. Forcing your daughter to marry a stranger and depriving her of education and everything else is not love or protection; it is an act of harsh punishment. Not knowing the difference between, protection, and abuse is another problem with some parents.

Of course you should correct or talk to your children when they do something wrong, but be gentle in your approach, and do not cause them any harm. My grandfather spanked me, and sometimes I received a stroke of a cane when I was young to correct my wrongdoing, but he did not do it to cause me any harm. At the time, that was his way of discipline. There were some, though, that used the same discipline method and caused their children harm and abused them.

Today, it is hands off any harsh punishment with wives and children in the civilized world. Such should prevail in every culture; parents should respect that. Most parents in undeveloped countries still believe that physical discipline is the best and most effective means of correcting children. Canes and other physical things were used by our parents and teachers as perfect tools to discipline children. In most cases, it was use in a way that did not cause harm. That is all changed now; it is now a crime to use this method to discipline children or anyone. Regardless, culturally in some societies, it is still their way of disciplining their wives and children, as they see this as the most effective way. They do not want to stop these practices, as they see it as losing power and control over their families. Hopefully, the new generation will change this in countries that hold on strongly to harmful traditional practices.

The new generations of young men that travel from Africa to the West are gradually closing the gap of forced marriages because they are practicing Western culture that values female children as much as male children and they treat both the same. But there are some men that grew up in Africa before coming to the West, and these men came with their traditional values and practices. For these men, you can take them away from African, but you cannot take the rigid African culture and tradition away from them.

As more of this generation's races are educating their female children, more girls are gaining independence and becoming financially stable. They are able to take control of their lives. Many are able to say no to forced marriages and also walk away from other abusive situations or circumstances.

What to Remember

Effective communication with your daughter and your family will go a long way to strengthen your relationship with them. Communication also includes good listening. Be a good listener, be patience, control your temper, and do not pass judgment, as this will prevent them from communicating freely with you.

If you show interest in what your children do or say, they will be closer to you and share their feelings with you without fear and will not keep secrets from you. Praise them for their hard work. If you praise your children for their hard work, you teach them how to praise and appreciate other people.

Parents with fewer children have better communication with their children. Also, a husband with one wife gives more attention to his family than men with plural wives and many children. Have the number of children you can truly attend to, because your attention is very important in their lives. Marry with love and have children when you are ready financially, morally, and physically and not because others are getting married or because a marriage is forced on you.

Some men marry because they feel they are old and big enough to do so. If you are old and big enough but lack the qualities of a mature man, your marriage may be problematic. However, you can learn these important qualities before you get married. As I said earlier, the size and age of a man does not determine his maturity, as maturity does not go with age.

Another problem with these men is that they have no idea how to deal with marital problems. They only follow in their fathers' footsteps, the only way they know growing up. If things are not working out well for them, they forever blame their attitude on their upbringing.

Some of these men compare notes with their fathers. I have heard some men say, "What is wrong with women these days? My father married more than one wife, and that was okay with the women." That may be true of your father in his day, but I don't think it was okay with the women. It only appeared okay because the women endured the pain and did not complain because no one would listen. Your father's days were so different than these days. You are not your father. Your father may have acted based on his lack of knowledge and lack of education, but these are your days. Accept and adapt to the changes of today. Live in the present and not in the past. As they say, "When you are in Rome, act like a Roman."

My grandfather once told me a story of why men married more than one wife and had many children. He said it was for children to help their parents with farm work (yam farm, cocoa farm, cassava farm, rubber plantation, and palm oil plantation). He said that the more children they had (especially male children), the larger and greater their farm was and the more money they got from their farm produce. The more women they had, the more children they had. Maintaining wives and children then was less expensive because life was not as complicated then as it is today, and people were content with their farm produce.

When male children were about to get married, their fathers would give them a piece of land to start their own farm. Some farmers became rich due to large-scale farming with help from their male children. The female children were very helpful to their mothers in cultivating the vegetables and doing the light farm work. This made sense at the time because farming and other hard-labor jobs needed lots of effort, especially in the days when most things were done manually.

But things are different now. Many parents do not farm anymore, and those who do are relying on the modern technology to do it. It does not need as much manual labor as it did them. Moreover, not many sons want to farm these days, especially as more and more boys are getting an education. Their priority is not farming anymore but other professions. If they do choose farming, they rely on modern ways to do it and not only manpower.

It is very important for a man to have a vision on how to lead his family. As they say, "a man without vision is worse than a blind man." Lots of men are in denial; some close their eyes to the truth and do not accept the fact that they are not mature enough to get married or lead a successful family. If you are a man with vision, you will lead a successful family.

A man with vision understands the needs of his family and plans ahead.
He provides good education for his children, including his female children.
He admits he is wrong and is willing to change.
He appreciates things in a marriage other than sex.
He makes right choices, even at difficult times.
He sets a goal for the future of his family and works hard to achieve his goal.

He does not subject his children and wife to hunger.
He compromises and puts his family's needs first.
He only has the number of children he can afford to care for.
He accepts change.
He teaches his children by example.
He conducts himself well on the inside, not only on the outside.
He treats others the way he wants to be treated.
He does not enslave his wife.
He provides equal treatment to both his male and female children.

In Africa, the poverty rate among children is very high. Most is due to lack of vision from their fathers. Many men marry more than one wife and have more children than they can care for. As a result, their children become beggars, street kids, uneducated kids, servants, prostitutes, armed robbers, and much more. Many men also depend on others (relatives, wives, churches, and government) to take care of their children, including paying school fees for their children; this is because they lack vision.

They cannot think ahead to realize that having many children comes with lots of responsibilities. Some fathers with many children are unable to care for their children's needs. They would become envious of others who have vision and planned ahead. Some become frustrated and put their frustrations on others around them, including their wives and children. When they asked people for help and could not get it, they got angry at the people. They have forgotten that you lie in your bed the way you made it. Such men cannot figure out why men with vision who have good jobs, a good family, fewer children, and one wife are progressing so much, and they are not. The answer is so simple; it is because the men with vision pursue other goals in life. They are not just busy having children and hoping that God will take care of their children, which is the wish of men without vision.

"God helps those who help themselves." God gave you choices; it is up to you to make the right choices. Remember that God is not your children's physical father; you are. God is their spiritual father. Therefore, you have to do all that is physical for them, while God directs you spiritually. Also remember that help does not fall from the sky. Goals can only be achieved if you work hard to achieve them. Be a visionary man, and your dream will come true for you. A man without vision does not achieve much.

A man without vision is without a future plan for his children.
He depends on his wife or others to raise his children.
He believes God will help him and does nothing to help himself.
He keeps having children without means to care for them.
He forces his children to marry for financial and material gain.
He knows what to say and does not know what to do.
He boasts of having children and has no idea how they grow up.
He keeps his distance from his children, just to avoid responsibilities.
He stays away from his children and watches from afar how others care for them.
He thinks the responsibility of raising his children is solely his wife's.
He thinks government handouts are all his children need.
He treats his family as his private property.
He acts like the master of castle.
He is abusive and controlling.

He deprives his children of education.
He boasts of what he is not to make himself look good before his friends.
He enslaves his wife.

You have to remember that everything you do has results. In these modern days, children need more than just a man as their father. They need a caring and visionary father. Be a father with vision

CHAPTER 33

What Has Changed

Rigid cultural values and beliefs are gradually changing among some African men, especially those born or raised in the Western world. Some men are adapting to the Western style of raising children. Western culture practices equal treatment for their male and female children.

Many young girls, boys, men, and women who traveled outside of Africa in search of better life are marrying people from different cultures with different beliefs. Many things that would not have been practiced or accepted in the old generation are gradually being introduced and accepted in some African societies.

Over the years, much has changed in societies and cities to narrow the gap in the way female and male children are treated by their fathers, but very little has been done in the villages to narrow the gap.

Many fathers now consider it beneficial to educate their daughters just the same way they do with their sons.

Many girls are now graduating from higher institutions and are securing positions in the workforce.

Most young women are able to combine working outside of the home and home chores successfully.

More African men are realizing that the family functions better with one wife, rather than plural wives.

With good education and people traveling from their countries to other parts of the world, many women and girls now have choices and are able to say no to forced marriages; they have the choice to choose their own husbands.

More men with plural marriages are treating their wives with some respect, regardless of the circumstances that led to such marriages.

There has been more awareness of the danger that girls and women of forced marriages face with their husbands.

More young girls, whether in the cities or villages, are more aware of the cultural torture they face and how this leads to abuse by their husbands, and they try to avoid it.

Some fathers are now allowing their children to travel to other parts of the world where different traditions are practiced and are accepting their children's change of attitude toward their traditions. If you allow your children to travel to the West or have brought them up in the West, you cannot take them away from the Western culture. There are some parents, however, who still strongly believe in their cultural and traditional practices and cannot see it any other way. They have negative attitudes toward other cultures.

Fathers who are educating their daughters are benefiting from their daughters in terms of happiness, love, closeness, and affection.

More African fathers are realizing that plural marriages are not necessarily the healthiest.

Many of these men are accepting that single families are happier than plural ones.

More daughters are able to talk with their fathers about anything or just to play or joke without being intimidated by him.

More fathers are friendlier and improving their relationships with their daughters, though some fathers are still noticeably distancing themselves from their daughters.

More men are now sharing responsibilities with their wives and are having happier marriages than those who are leaving their responsibilities to their wives or controlling their wives.

More fathers are now considering the financial, physical, and moral responsibility of raising children before getting married and more fathers are having fewer children, so they can provide for them.

CHAPTER 34

What to Consider

If your plan is to force your daughter into marrying a man she does not love, have a change of attitude, as this is not the best for her. Consider investing in her education instead. Do not consider your daughters as your source of income or the way out of your poverty. If you give your daughters a good education, just as your sons, and show them equal love, they will grow up into happy women and will make you proud in the end.

If you do not educate your daughter, she may end up as a servant in her husband's house. If your reason for forcing your daughter to marry some stranger, a man old enough to be her father or grandfather, is to get a big dowry from your in-law and perhaps to enrich yourself, you may be making a big mistake. Your in-law may give you a big dowry and may give you some money initially to settle your immediate debts. That may be all you will get from your in-law, which is not enough to make you rich. You may only be putting your daughter in danger, and your poverty will resurface at the end.

Remember that educated women are more respected than the illiterate women by their husbands and the society at large. If your daughter chooses suicide rather than staying in the unhealthy marriage, as it is in some cases, you will end up losing your daughter altogether; and your hope for wealth from your in-laws will also end. Think of the benefit that education will bring to your daughter and to you, and make the right choice to educate her.

Times have changed. You need to adjust to the new changes. You need to realize that some things that were allowed and accepted in your day, growing up, are no longer acceptable in this modern day. Women are now able to own their own houses, buy and drive a vehicle, and other things that were impossible in your day. What a man can do, a woman can do better. Give your daughter the chance to be the woman she wants to be.

If most African men would believe in their wives and respect them the way they respect their mothers, marriages would be more successful and children would be happier and grow into happy adults. Some men believe that the only woman they can trust and respect is their mother. Your wife can never be your mother or replace your mother, but remember she is a mother to your children, so treat her with the respect she deserves, regardless of how you marry her.

Whether you marry by choice, by arrangement, or to a woman who was forced on you for marriage or given to you as a gift, once you agree to live with her as your wife, you must respect her, love her, and honor her, just as you love yourself. This is God's command. Your wife should not be treated as your slave and your daughter as your servant. "Be a godly husband, as a godly husband will have a blessed marriage."

Many children who grow up in polygamous homes are more secretive and less trusting. Sometimes they are manipulative and are more close-minded than children brought up in a monogamous home. If you grew up in polygamy and lived a secret life, learn to be open, as openness is a key to trust.

Be a clear mirror that you want your children to look at, because children act what they see. They may want to marry someone of your kind when they decide to marry. I have seen some cases where children refuse to marry because of their experiences at home with their fathers and mothers. They do not want to be treated the way their fathers treat their mothers. Your behavior with your wife may send a wrong message to them, and they may think that all men are the same. Act more than you speak because "action speaks louder than words."

Ask for your wife's assistance to teach your daughter good behavior, because when it comes to parenting, women know best. Teach your children good manners from when they are young, as lessons taught to a child stay with them until later years.

Consider your economic, mental, emotional, and physical state before having children. If your situation does not enable you to have children, do not have them, as children should never be neglected, abandoned, or sold for any reason. Once you have children, they should be part of your family for life, and your responsibilities for them should be for a long time, until they grow up to be a man or woman and are able to make their own decisions. If you engage your wife in this task, you will get good results from your children.

CHAPTER

35

Be a Supportive Wife and Mother

home cannot run smoothly without the effort of both husband and wife. Be your husband's rock, as he should be your rock. Don't look for a perfect attitude from your husband, because nobody is perfect. Work with him at his own level. It takes lots of effort, commitment, compromise, understanding, self-control, love, trust, and faithfulness to be a good and supportive wife. In the end, it is worth the effort.

For your husband to sincerely show his unconditional love and respect to you, you must be able to perform all your duties as a wife and mother, including showing him love, believing in him, trusting him, listening to him, and appreciating him, just as husband is expected to be to his wife.

Being an educated career woman does not take away your role as a woman and a mother; it only modifies your role. You still have to fulfill your obligation to your husband and to your children. Your husband cannot do it alone without difficulty, but with you, things will be a lot easier, as they say, "two heads are better than one".

The Bible describes the wife as "a complement" of her husband. "The Lord God said, "It is not good for a man to be alone. I will make a helper suitable for him" (Genesis 2:18). As such, she supplies important qualities to the marriage. And as his complement, she does not compete with him but gives him loving support, thus promoting peace within the family. "Let wives be in subjection to their husband" (Ephesians 5:22). What, though, if she disagrees with him on matters? In that case she should feel free to express her opinions in a dignified and respectful manner, just as she would like her husband to speak to her.

"Wives submit yourselves unto your husbands, as it is fit in the Lord. Husbands love your wives, and do not be bitter against them" (Colossians 3:18–19). Husbands must receive the respect and love shown to them by their wives with gratitude and treat them as fragile as a broken plate. First Peter 3:7 says, "In the same way, husbands must live with your wives with proper understanding that they are the weaker sex." Treat them with respect, because they also will receive together with you God's gift of life. Do this so that nothing will interfere with your prayer.

Marriage should be a two-way street; give and take. "Let the husband render to his wife her due, but let the wife also like wise to her husband" (Corinthian 7:3–4). "The husband should fulfill his marital duty to his wife, and likewise the wife to her husband. The wife does not have authority over her own body but yield it to her husband. In the same way, the husband does not have authority over his own body but yields it to his wife."

You have to recognize the red flags of an unhealthy marriage. If your kindness, loyalty, and unconditional love is not good enough for your husband, and he is taking you for granted, abusing you, and disrespecting you, seek help for him and for yourself and address the issues as soon as possible; better sooner than later, as abusive husbands have no boundaries. After seeking help and it fails, and he continues to be abusive toward you, you can then decide if the marriage is for you. "It is better to be safe than sorry."

Remember that you cannot force love; it should be natural. All you can do is your best and hope your best is good enough to sustain your marriage. You cannot do more than your best. As a woman you are unique and have an amazing strength, regardless of what your controlling husband may want you to believe.

What are women's strengths?

- They have strength that amazes the world
- They hold the keys that open all doors
- They bear hardships and carry burdens but hold happiness, love, and joy
- They fight for justice, but most times they go without so their family can have
- They are mothers of the world
- They make their environment safe for their children
- They bear the pain of pregnancy and smile through the pain and joy of childrearing
- They love unconditionally
- They put others' needs before theirs
- They smile and sing when soothing their babies, even when they are not happy
- They care for those who do not even care for them.
- They forgive easily
- They don't give up hope
- They are the strength of their families
- They are the best teachers
- They shine lights on their homes when clouded with darkness

Blessings to the young and old caught up in forced marriages who are struggling in many ways, either to make peace with their circumstances or to find their way out of the ugly situations. I hope that help will come their way sooner rather than later.

In your struggles, remember:

- You are not alone
- Your stay here on earth is not by accident
- Hold on to your strength
- Hope for a better tomorrow
- Hold on to your faith and believe that God never fails
- God has a purpose for you

- God will open a door for you
- The door God opens will never close
- Do not choose death over life

Read, believe, and have faith in yourself because faith never fails.

Believe in yourself.

You did not choose to be born. God knows why he created you.

Believe there is a purpose for your being.

Even when you are discriminated against by men, believe that you are equal in the sight of God.

You may not be who they want you to be, but there is a reason why you are different.

If all flowers were roses, there would be no lilies.
Don't mourn your past experiences. God knows why you were chosen to experience it.

Know that living in the past will not strengthen the future, so work hard for a better future.

You have a story to tell today because of yesterday's experience, so every disappointment can be a blessing.

Without an event, there is no story to tell.

You may have been chosen to make a difference. Work hard to make the difference.

Believe tomorrow will be better than yesterday for all helpless women. Do your part to make a difference.

Believe in your inner beauty, no matter what others tell you.

Move forward, as you cannot turn back the hands of time.

Live in the moment because life is a gift.

If you make mistakes at times because you are not perfect, see it as opportunity to learn and grow.

Listen to other people's advice and not just what you think, because it is never too late to learn.

Believe no one can predict your future. It will come as a surprise.

Believe in a heart of forgiveness, as God forgave us all.

Let go of your anger of yesterday, and face tomorrow with courage.

Appreciate your existence, for God never makes mistakes.

You may not be able to change others, but you can change yourself.

Stop asking why you do not have everything you want, and make use of what you have.

Bear no grudges for those who discriminated against you because they don't know any better.

Have a heart of gold because gold never fades.

What cannot be changed can be endured.

Save a girl.

If you cannot save many, please save a girl. Donate and support those fighting hard to make a difference in the lives of girls forced to marry. When you save one girl, you may have saved many. As the saying goes, "Educate a man, and you educate an individual. Educate a woman, and you educate the nation."

Without your help and the help of many organizations out there that are already fighting to stop forced marriages, nothing may change. Play your part, and leave the rest to others. A single drop of water makes a mighty ocean.

If you are keeping a girl or wife (or wives) against her will, set them free so that God will forgive you for any wrong you have done towards them. Consider changing your behavior; a negative attitude brings negative results.

CHAPTER 36

Questions for Fathers

1. Are you a father who only punishes your children when they make mistakes and doesn't reward them when they have done well?

2. Do you only use physical or psychologically cruel methods to correct your children's wrongdoing?

3. Do you implement harsh punishment on your children without consulting with your wife?

4. Do you always yell and hit your children as a way to get messages through to them?

5. Do you want your children to do as you say and not as you do?

6. Do you always fight in front of your children but get upset when they are involved in a fight?

7. Are you mean to your wife, but expect better treatment for your daughter when she is married?

8. Are you a father who does not provide food for your children but expects them to be well fed?

9. Are you a father who does not pay school fees for his children but expects them to be first in class?

10. Are your children ashamed to call you their father because of your attitude?

11. Do you want your son to be a good man, but you do not show him by your actions what a good man should be?

12. Are you a father who is never there for his children and who left the responsibilities of raising your children to your wife?

13. Are you a father who does not provide clothing for your children, but expect them to be well dressed?

14. Are you a father who keeps secrets from your wife, but expect your wife to be honest with you?

15. Are you a father with children from different women, as many as you can, and you expect the government to take care of them?

16. Are you a father who plays games with friends for hours every day, even after work, and forgets that your family needs you at home?

17. Are you a father who does not provide money for his wife and expects her to cook the best food for you?

18. Are your children afraid of you?

If you answer yes to most of the questions above, it means you have a lot to work on. However, it is not too late to change. Live in the present, let yesterday be history, and face tomorrow with courage. Don't be left out of the present, and don't close the door to the future.

Treat your children with love. Having a good father should not have to be a game of luck; it should be a child's right.

Be a clear mirror in which your daughter sees the type of man she would want to marry. Your daughter will remember the way you treat her and her mother when she was young and may make her decision on men because of that. If your treatment of her and others was good, she will look for the same treatment from a man. If your treatment was bad, it may be a turning point for her. Teach by your actions and not only by your words.

Conclusion

N o children should have to choose death over life, and no children or women should be forced to marry men they do not love. No children should ever be forced to marry a man with plural wives or a man old enough to be their father or grandfather. The right to choose their own husbands at the right time should be given to them. If your daughter stays in a forced marriage, it does not mean she is happy. She may be staying for other reasons.

Despite the negative impact that forced marriages have on girls and women and the fact that some hundreds of young girls and women are choosing suicide to escape forced marriages, some parents still continue to force their children into marriages. They believe that male children can be trusted to care for their parents, later in life and to preserve their family fortune. But this is not always the case. Some women are more responsible and better at managing their family business than some men; this is a proven fact in lots of cases.

If fathers would trust their daughters and empower them as they do their sons, the whole family would be happier. Not all male children are responsible; lots of female children are more responsible than male children. Teach and model to your female children what they are to expect from their future husbands. Treat them as you would want other men to treat them, and treat their mother in the same way.

Be disciplined, as it takes a disciplined father to be able to discipline his children. No one says it is an easy job, but there is no price tag in raising children. Again, it is your choice to have them. Children do not ask to be born; if you choose to have them, you have to be ready to handle the responsibilities that come with raising them.

Praise and respect all women because they are worthy to be praised for their strength; blessings to all the men that respect women.

Be a man with vision. Don't be blind to situations surrounding your wife and children. A man without vision is considered a blind man.